MACKINAC
Island

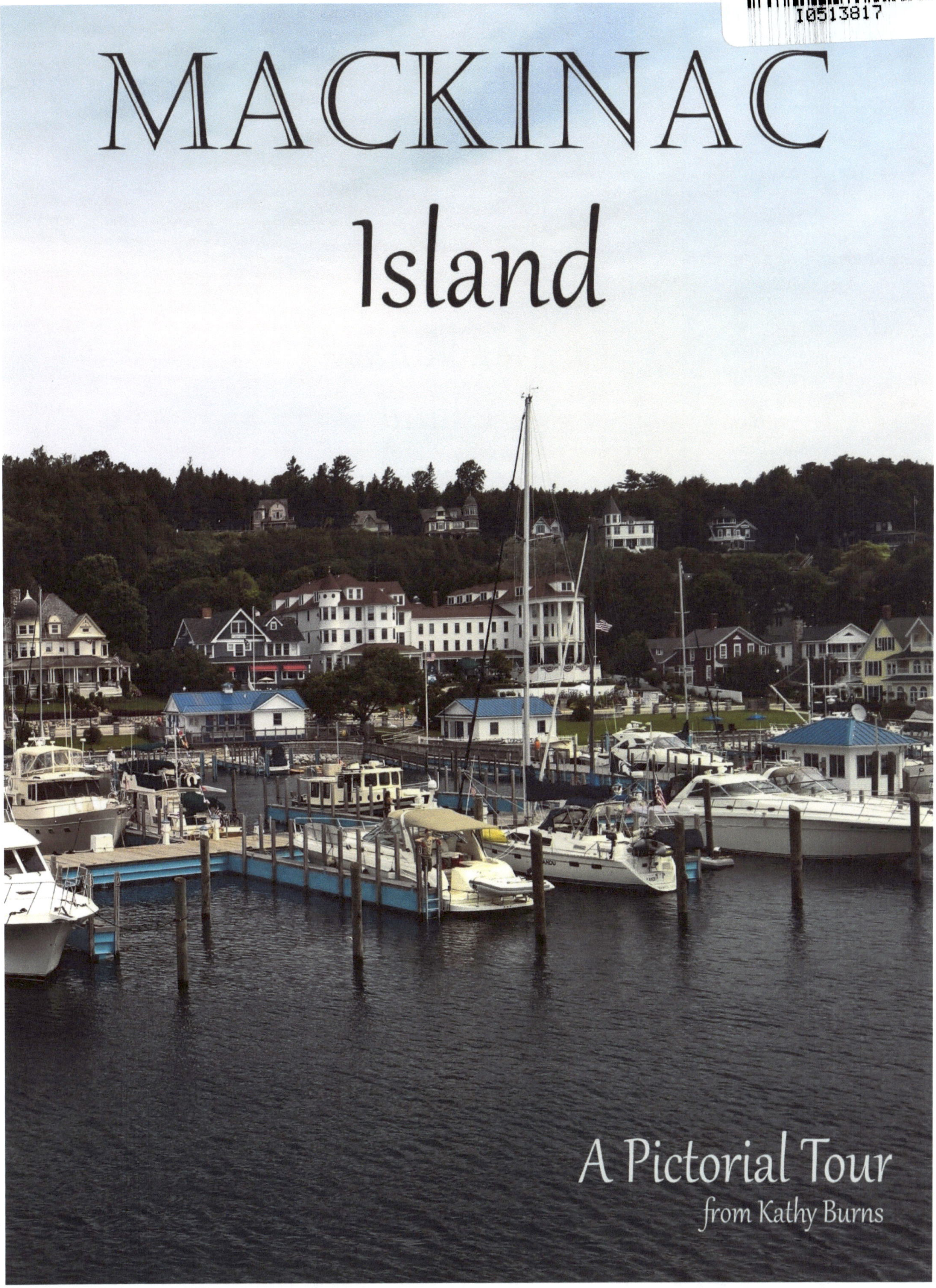

A Pictorial Tour
from Kathy Burns

Mackinac Island

Pictorial Travel Notes & Tour

By Kathy Burns

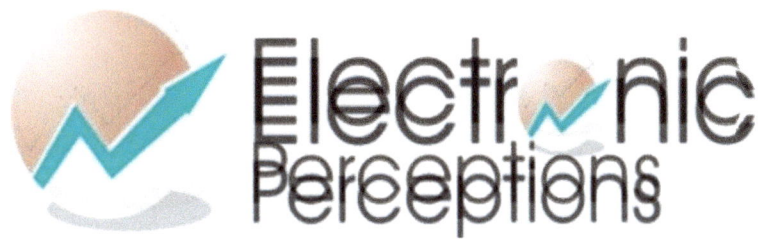

Electronic Perceptions
www.ElectronicPerceptions.com
©2018 Kathy Burns

Copyright

This electronic booklet is copyrighted ©2018 Kathy Burns. All rights are reserved.

Unless otherwise noted, photos in this book are ©2017, Kathy Burns.

This book may not be disassembled, decompiled, changed, copied, or otherwise taken apart for other uses. The photos are for the editorial purposes of this publication only, and are not licensed for any other use online or off.

You may not give this book away, share it with others, sell it, or otherwise distribute it without the proper authorization. Authorization is only available directly from the author.

Small excerpts may be used for reviews and commentary.

This book is for informational and entertainment purposes only. Nothing contained herein should be considered as legal, financial, or professional advice.

Introduction

Mackinac (pronounced MAK-in-aw) Island is a gorgeous tourist and historical spot in Michigan. I got the chance to visit the island with family in the summer of 2017 and had a blast. This book is a travel essay of sorts, containing photos from the perspective of a first-time visitor to the island.

I had no prior knowledge of the place, other than it had been the movie set location for a movie I loved when I was younger: "Somewhere in Time". The movie starred Christopher Reeve and Jane Seymour, and featured several locations from the Island, including The Grand Hotel.

I was wholly unprepared for the breadth of things to do and see when I visited the island. It is a treasure trove of historical information, preserved skills, and just plain fun.

This travel snippets book doesn't even begin to feature the wonderful foods and other activities that can be found on the island. I look forward to visiting many more times, to capture some of those themes.

I hope you enjoy this pictorial tour, and that it inspires you to add this destination to your family's future travel list!

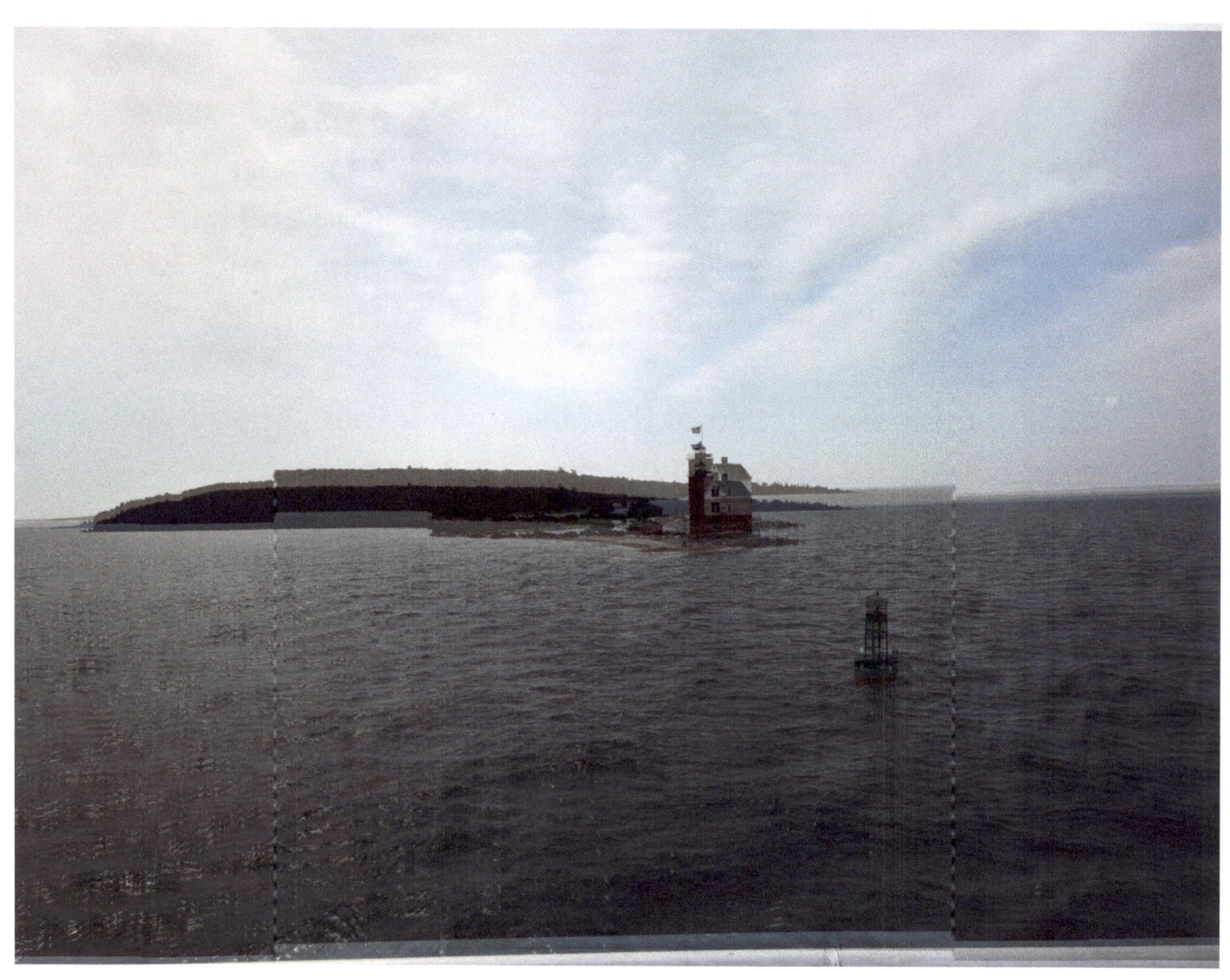

To get to the island, you must board a ferry and ride it across the lake. When I was there, you could choose an expedited ferry or a regular one. According to the official website, you can also take a small charter flight.

The image above shows a small lighthouse and buoy, partway across the lake.

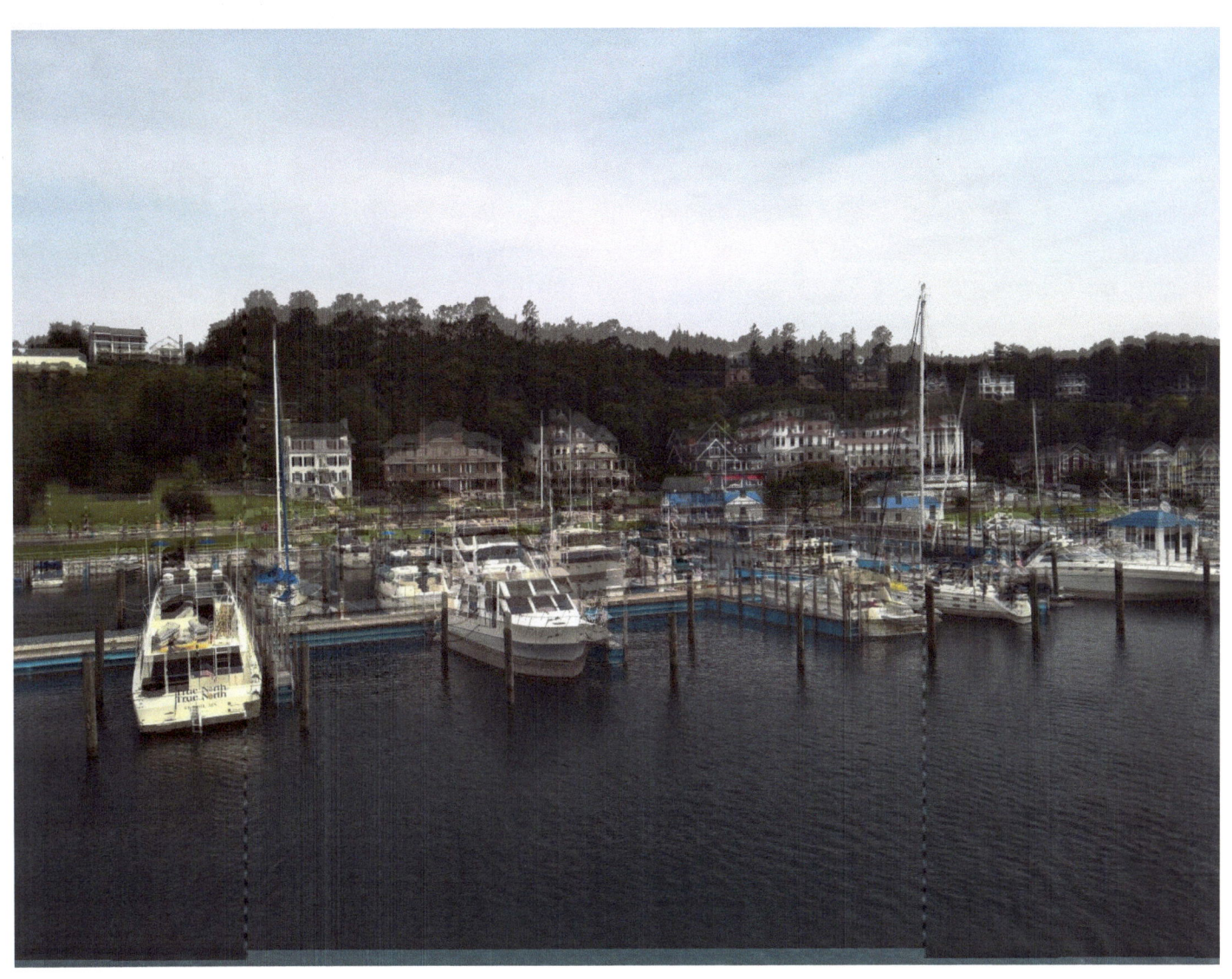

As the ferry is pulling into the dock, you can see a beautiful view of the boat harbor on the island.

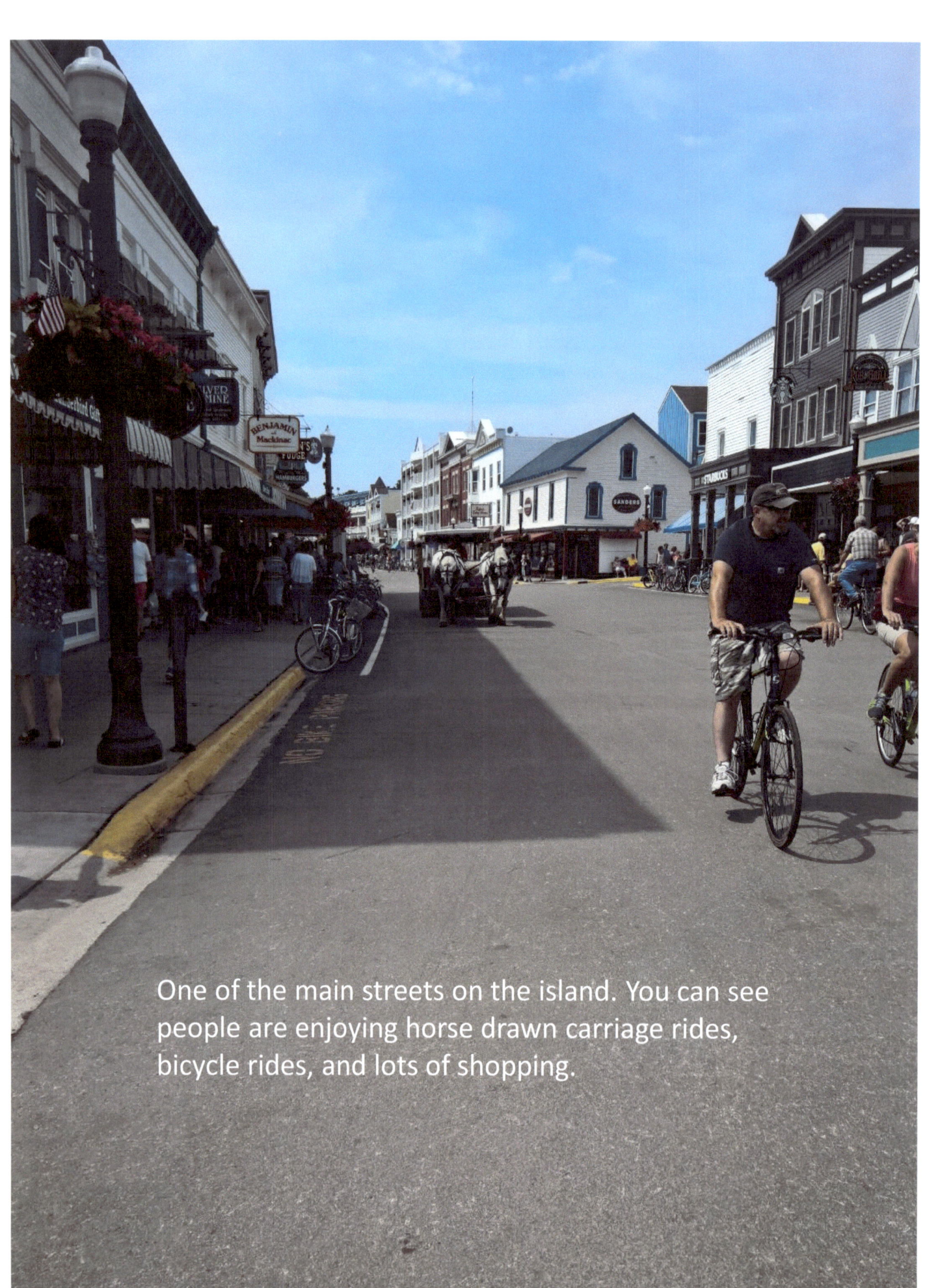

One of the main streets on the island. You can see people are enjoying horse drawn carriage rides, bicycle rides, and lots of shopping.

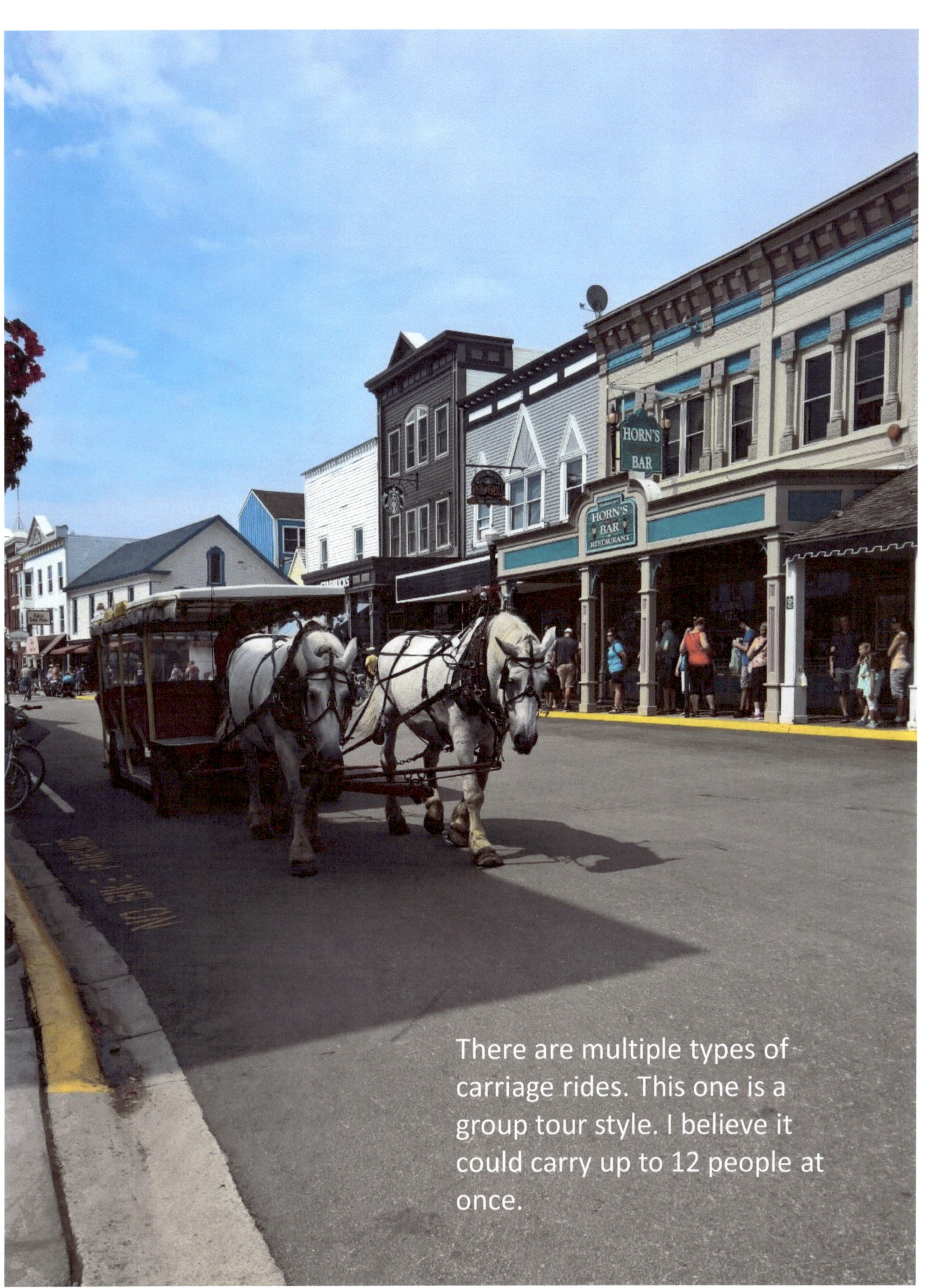

There are multiple types of carriage rides. This one is a group tour style. I believe it could carry up to 12 people at once.

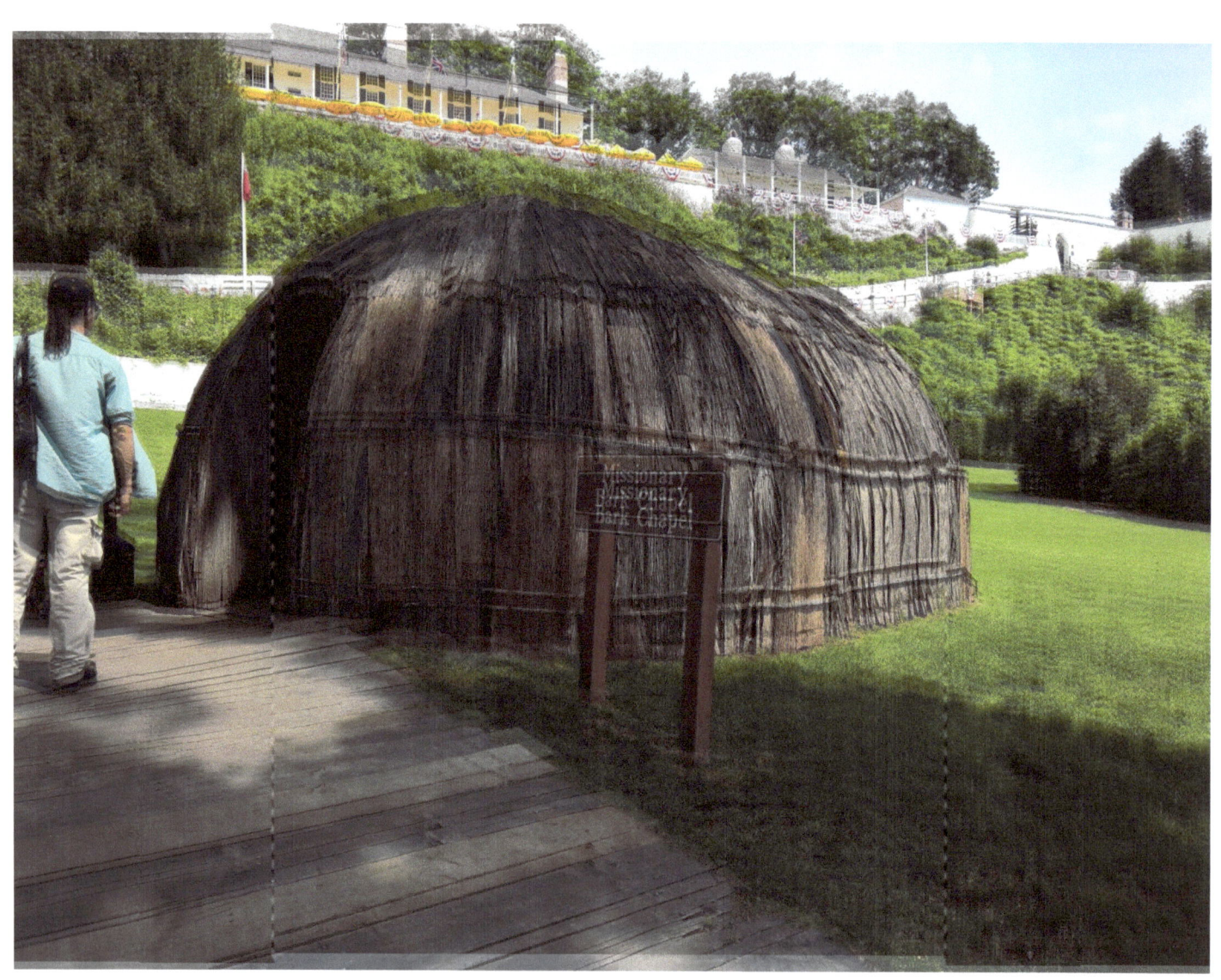

This was some sort of primitive chapel made of sticks or thatch. I believe there is historical significance to it, but unfortunately it was busy when I was there, so I never found out anything about it.

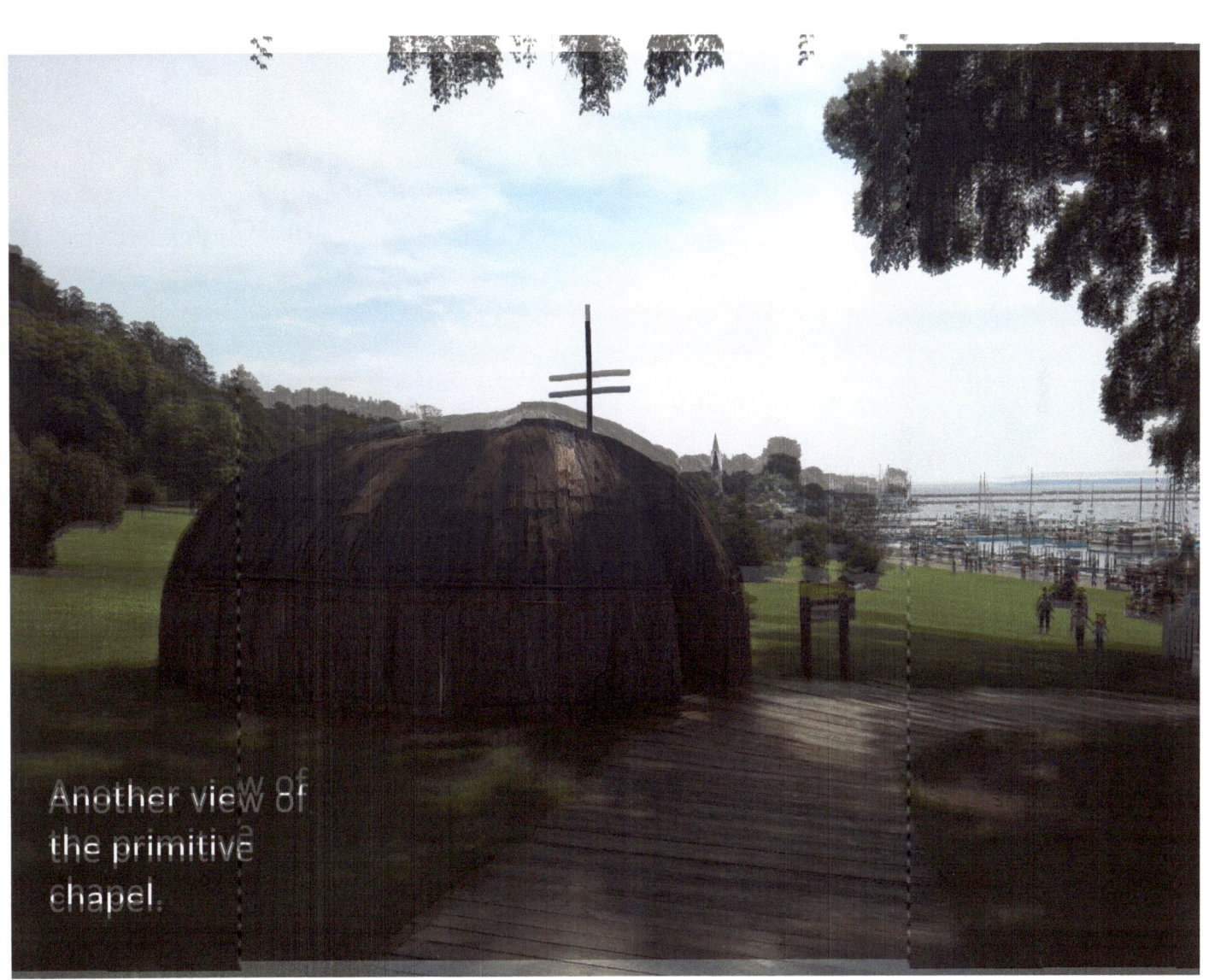
Another view of the primitive chapel.

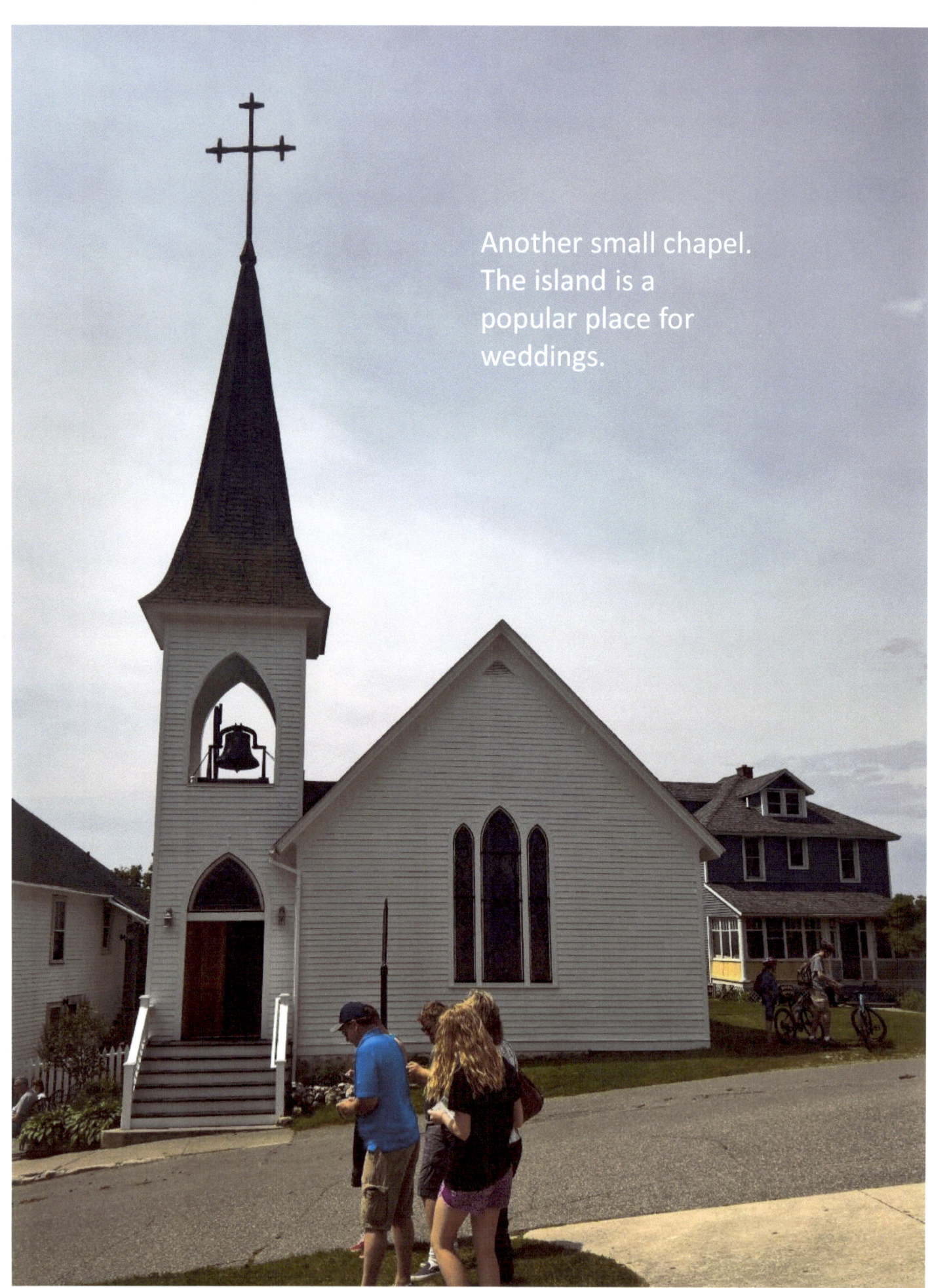

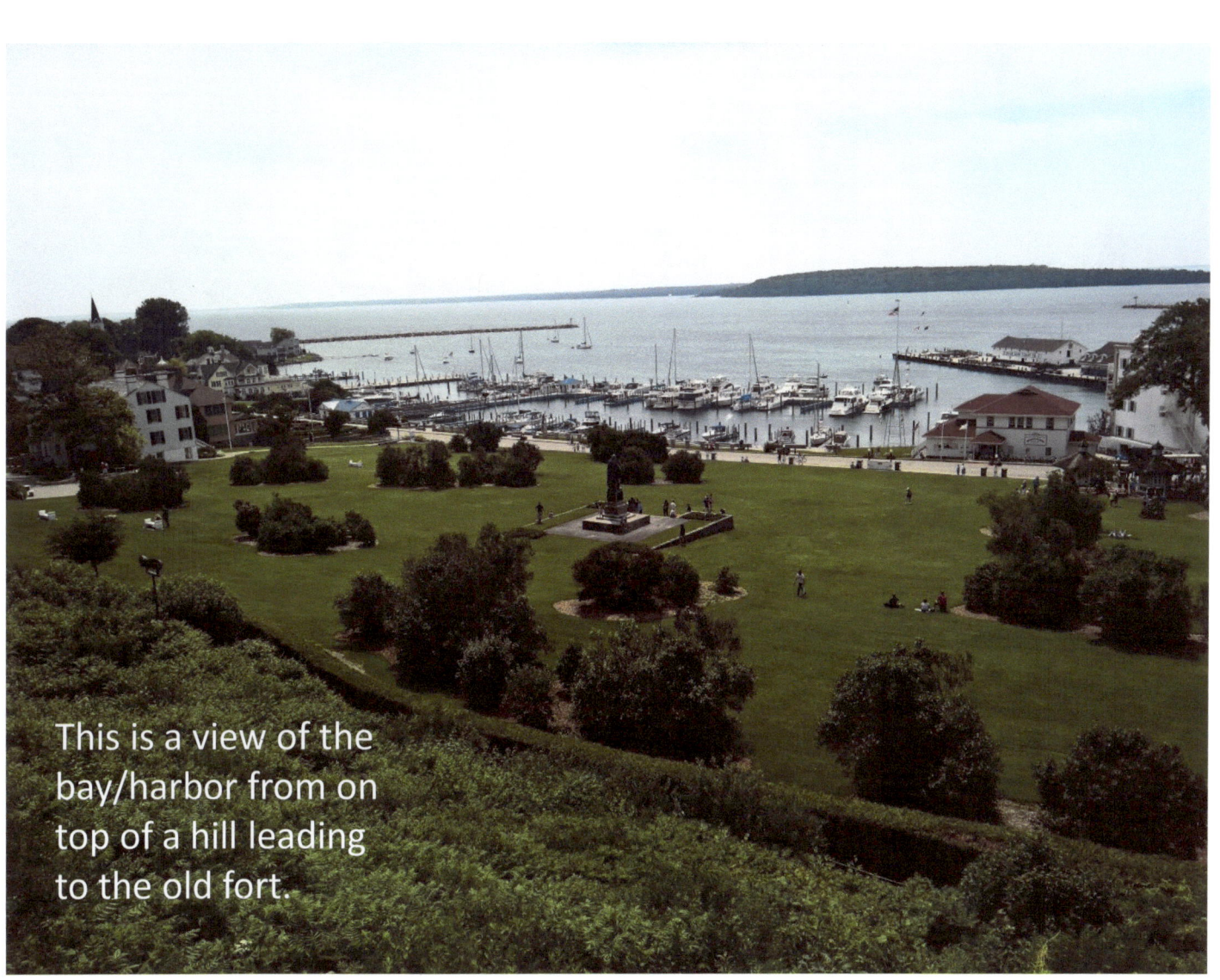

This is a view of the bay/harbor from on top of a hill leading to the old fort.

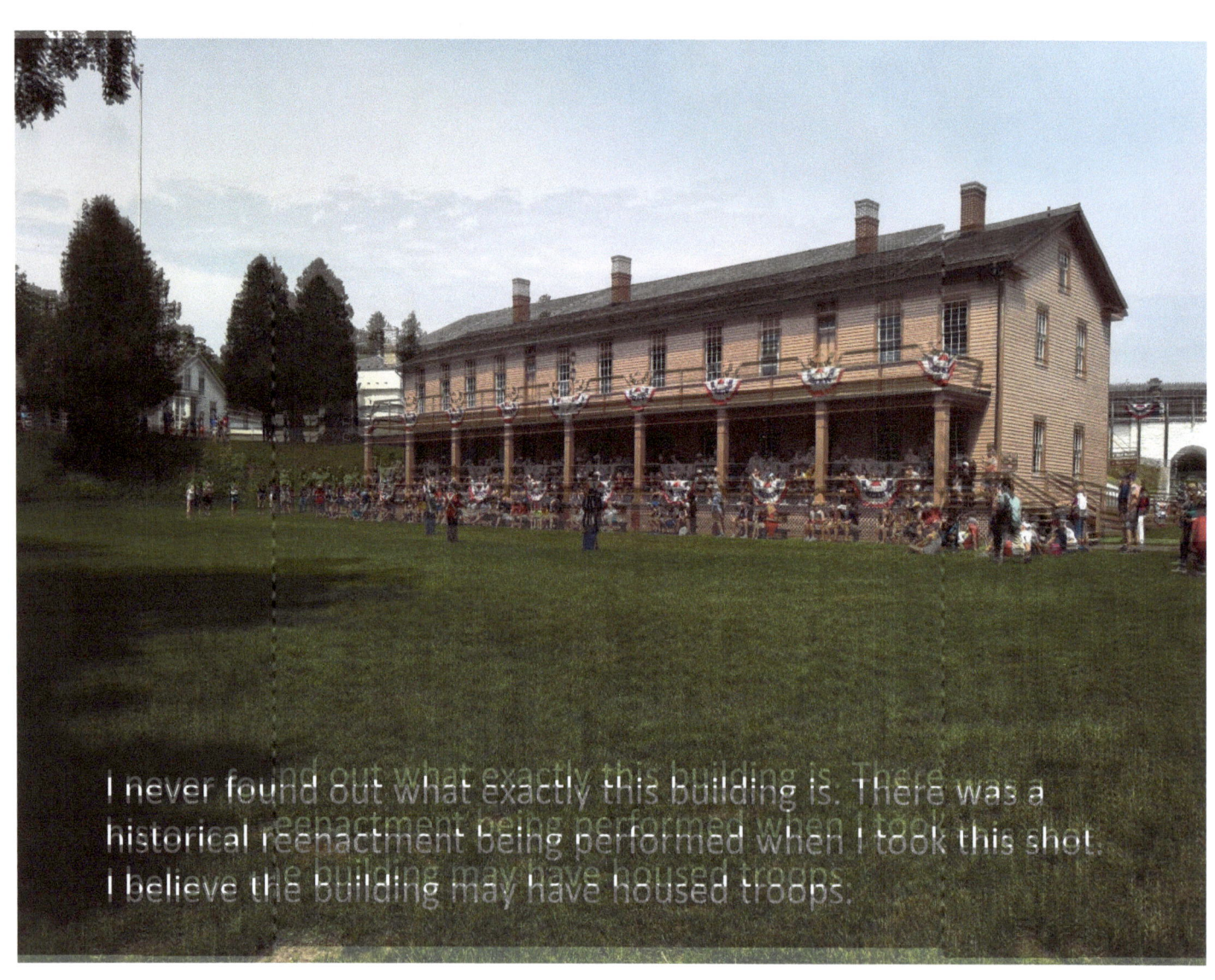

I never found out what exactly this building is. There was a historical reenactment being performed when I took this shot. I believe the building may have housed troops.

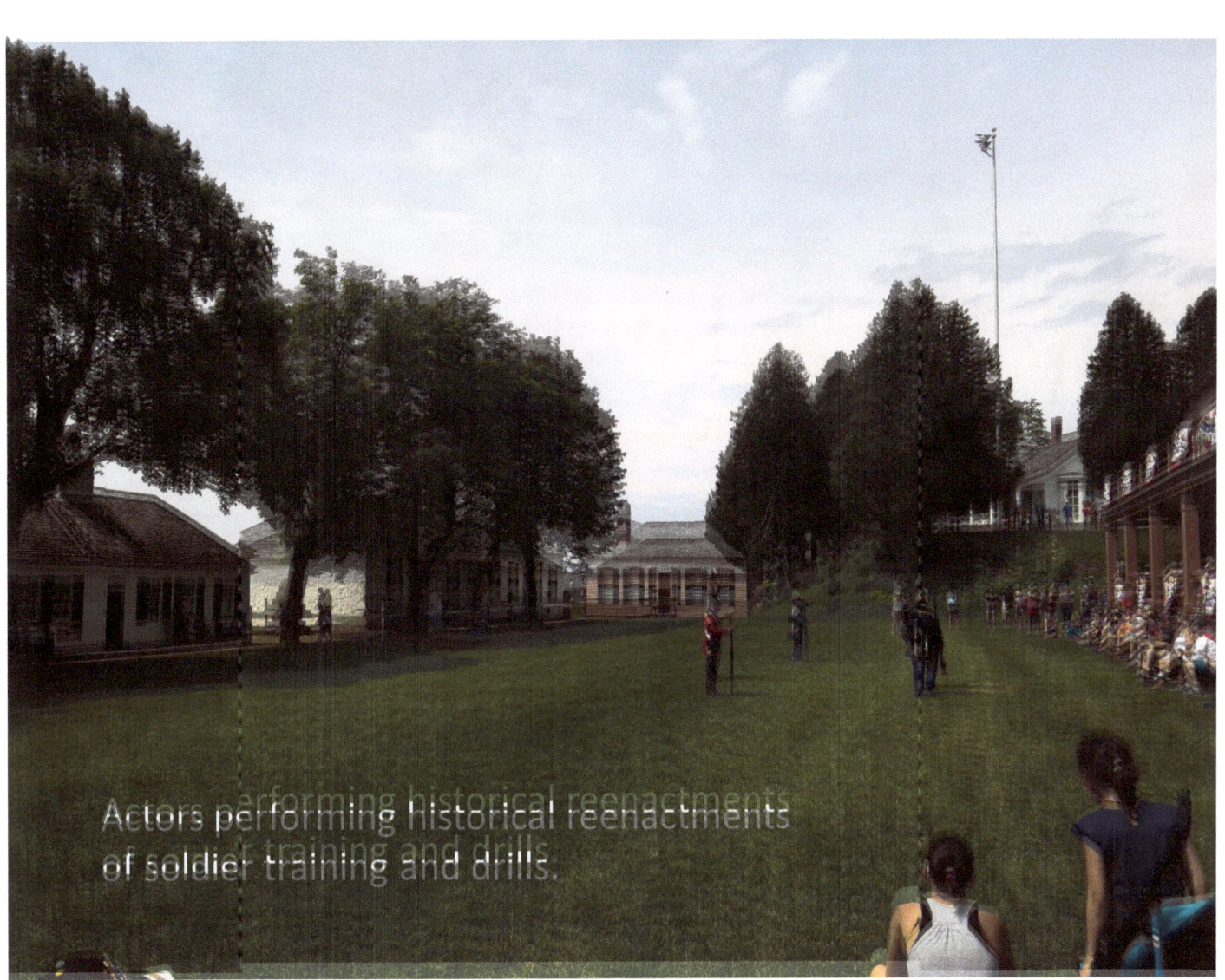
Actors performing historical reenactments of soldier training and drills.

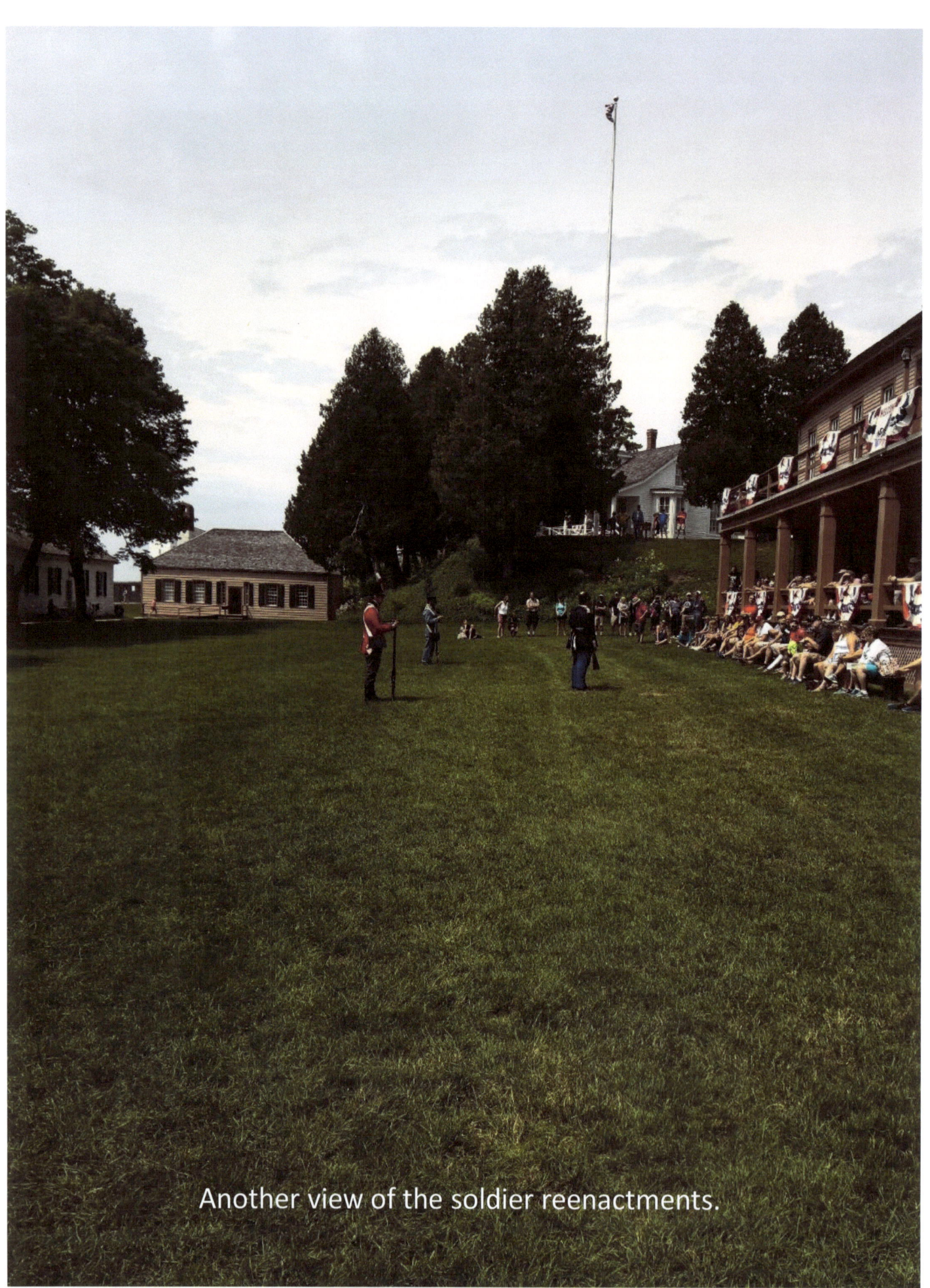
Another view of the soldier reenactments.

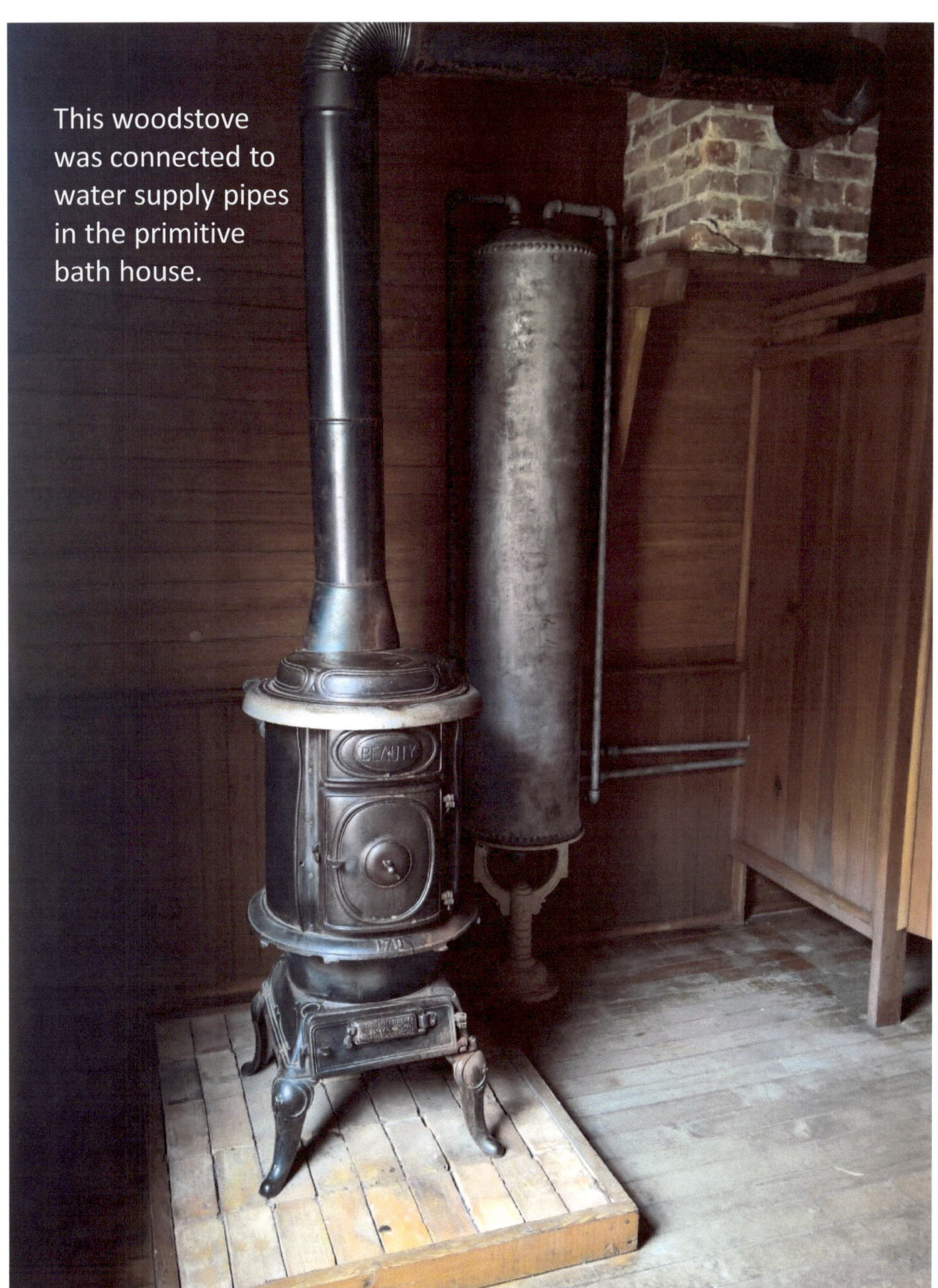

This woodstove was connected to water supply pipes in the primitive bath house.

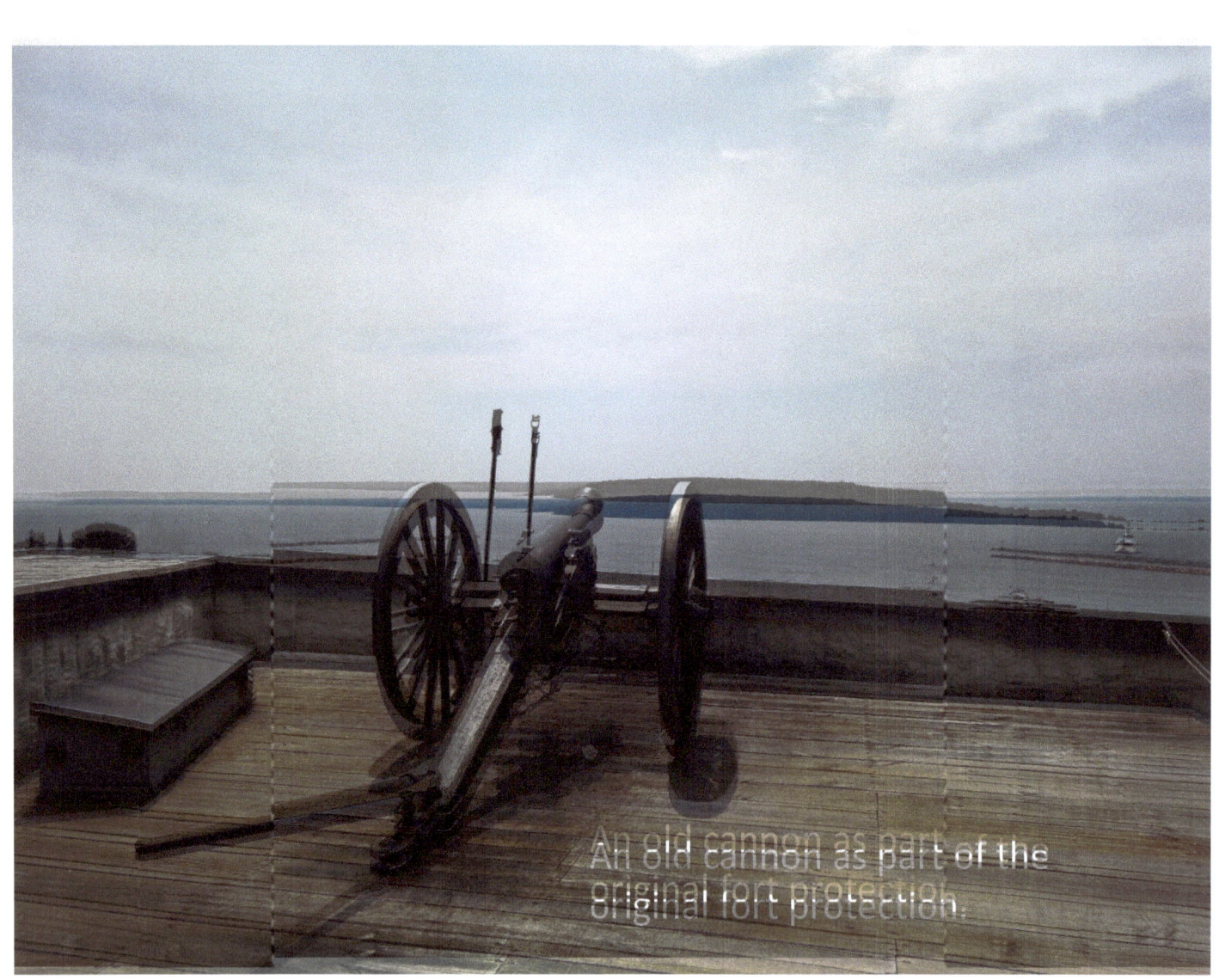
An old cannon as part of the original fort protection.

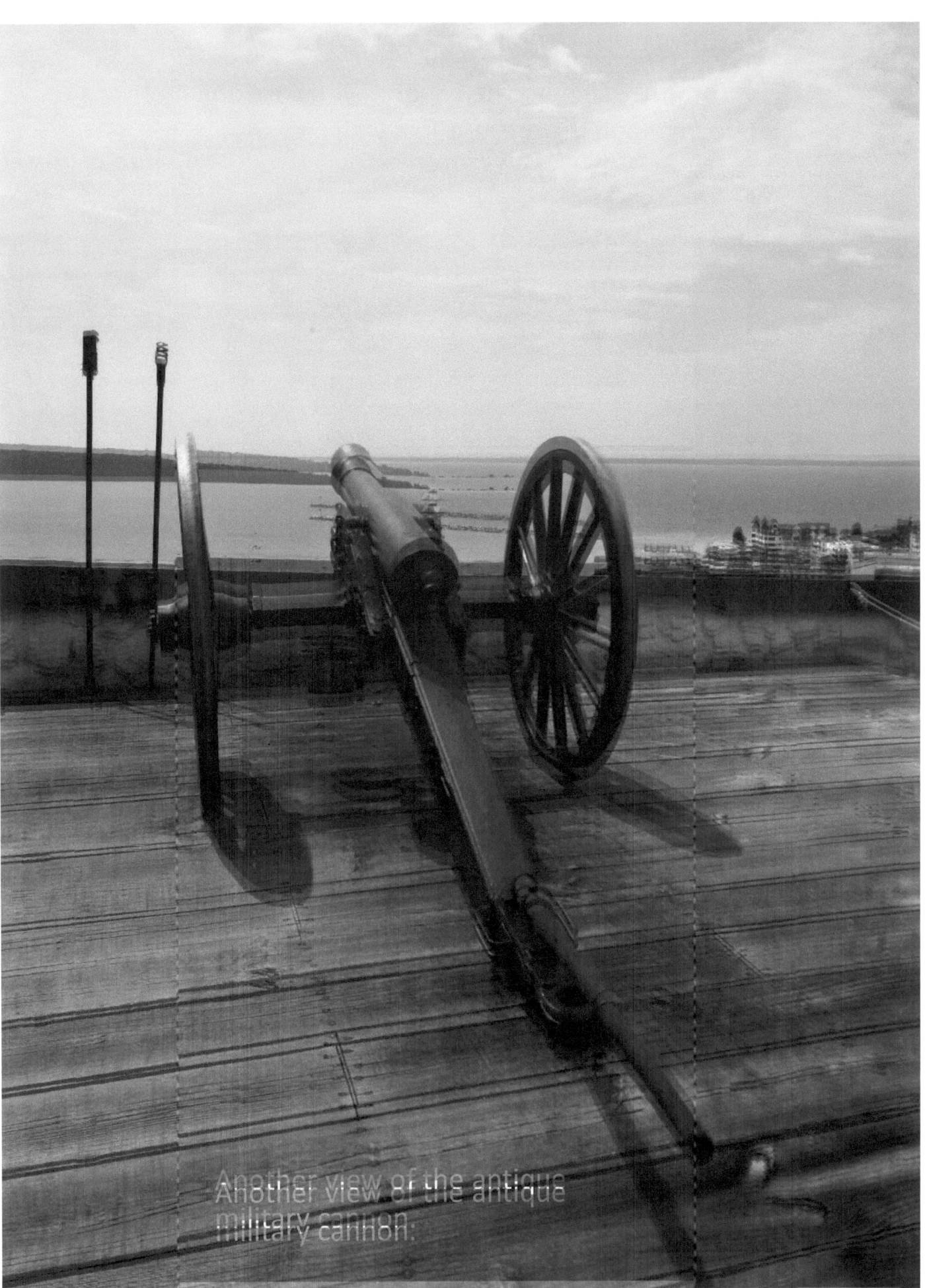

Another view of the antique military cannon.

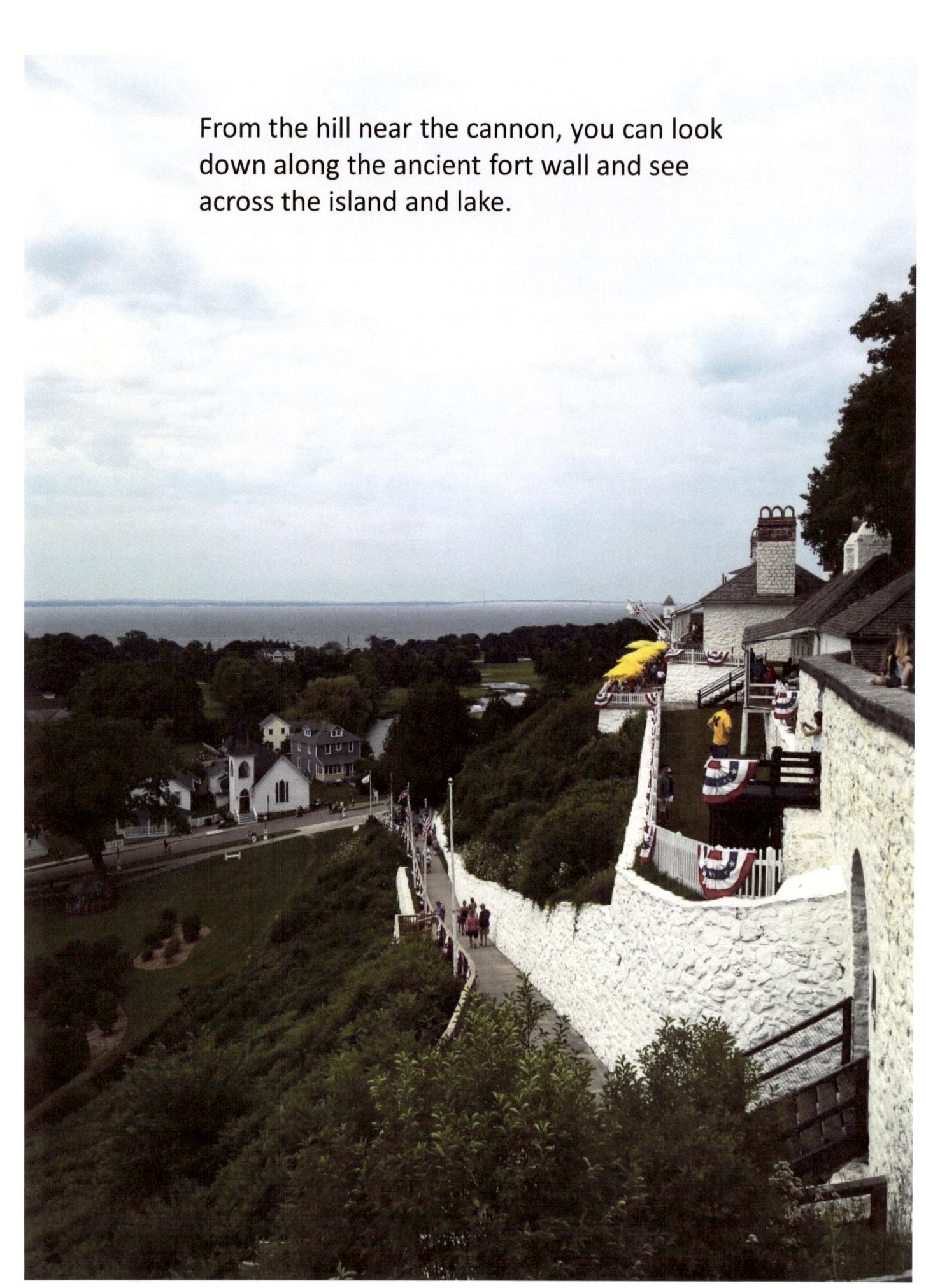

From the hill near the cannon, you can look down along the ancient fort wall and see across the island and lake.

Another view of the fort wall and the view from the cannon position.

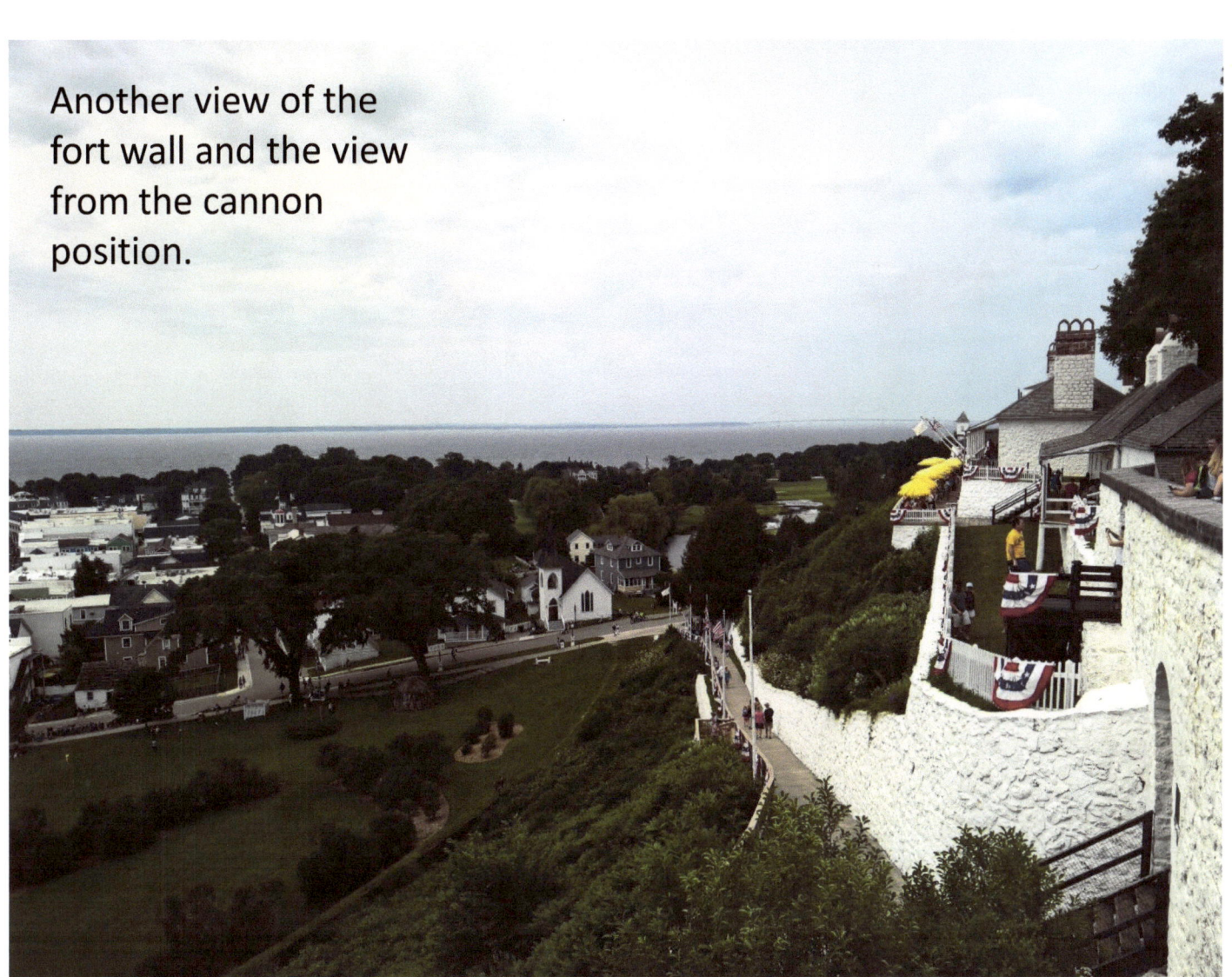

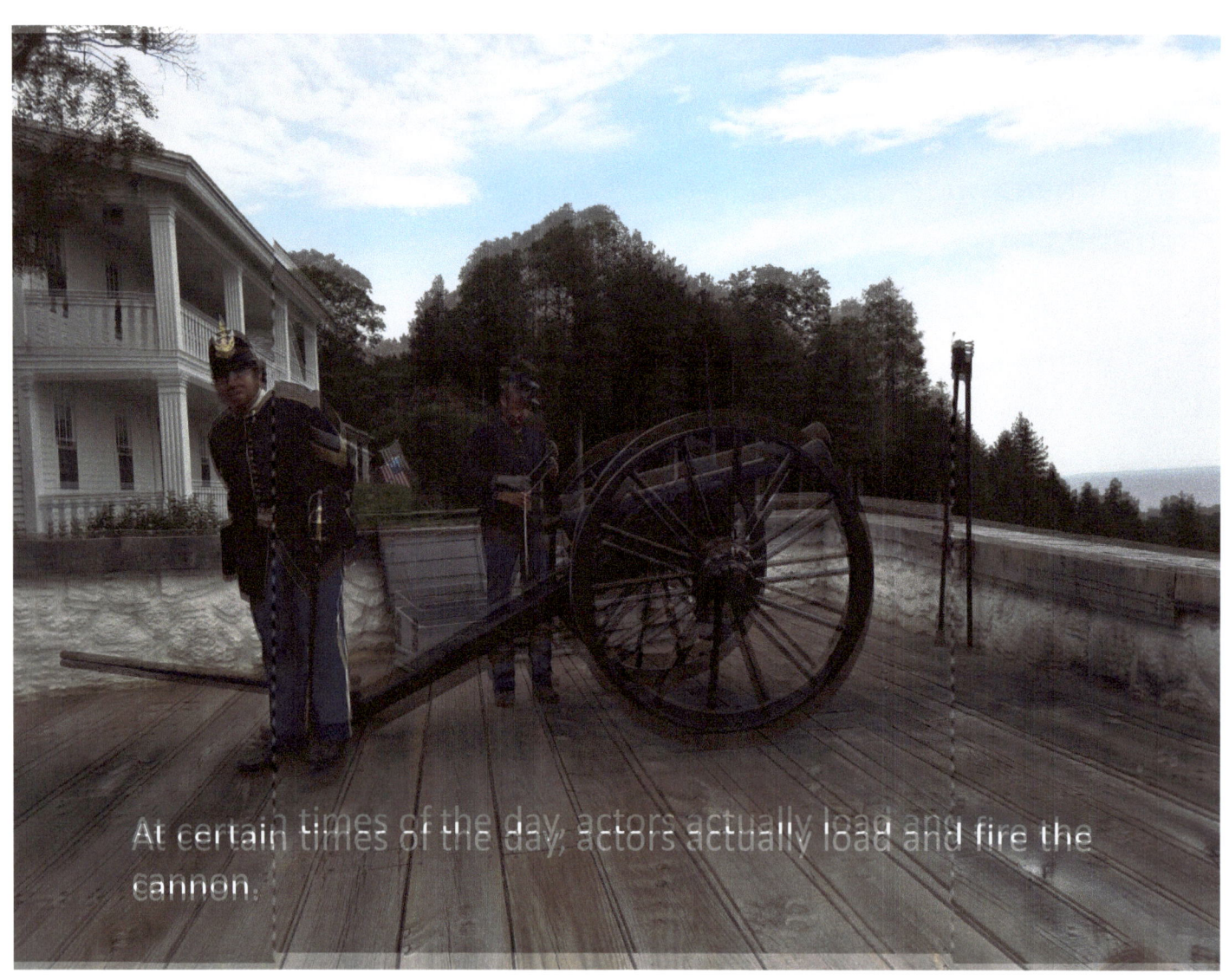
At certain times of the day, actors actually load and fire the cannon.

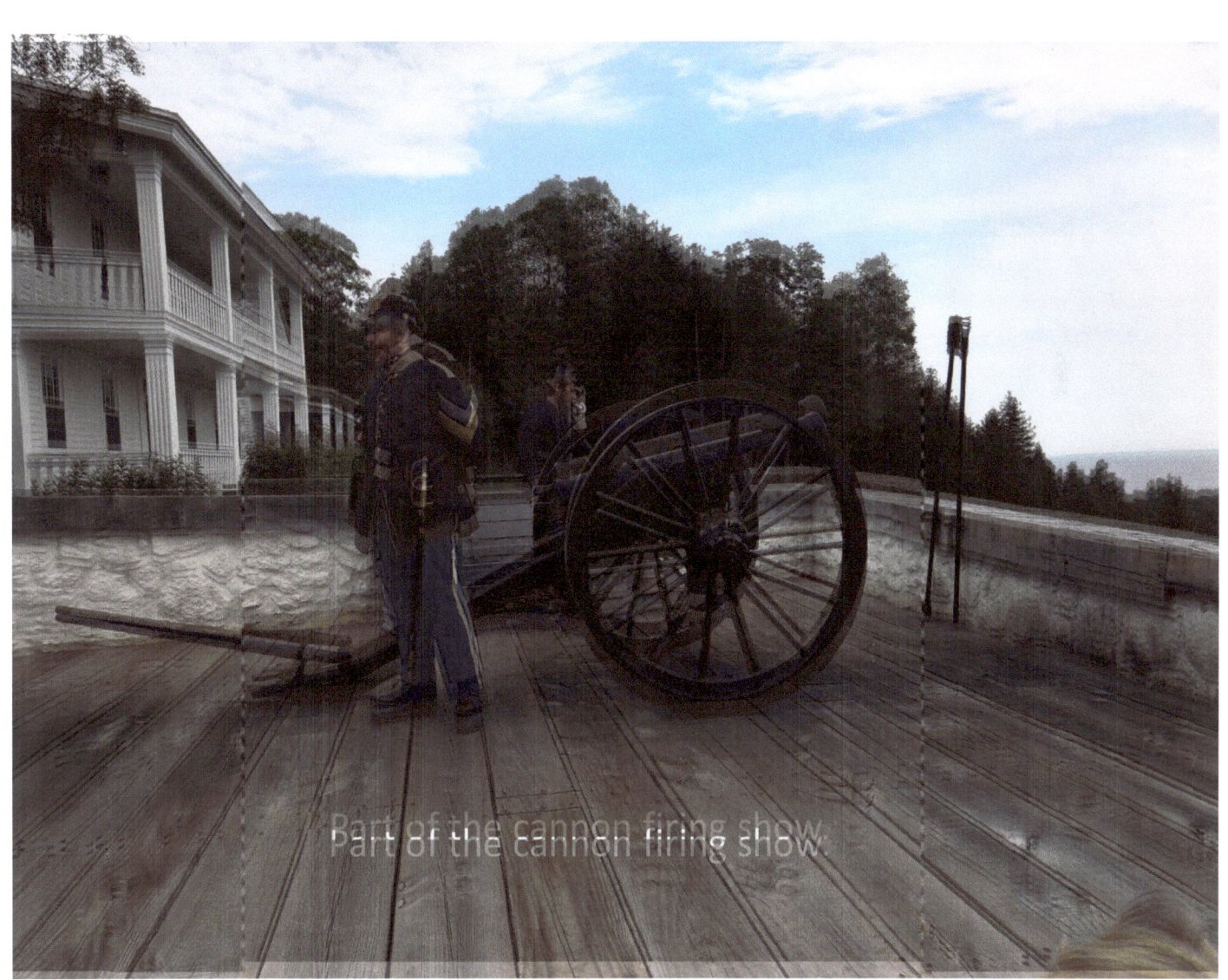
Part of the cannon firing show

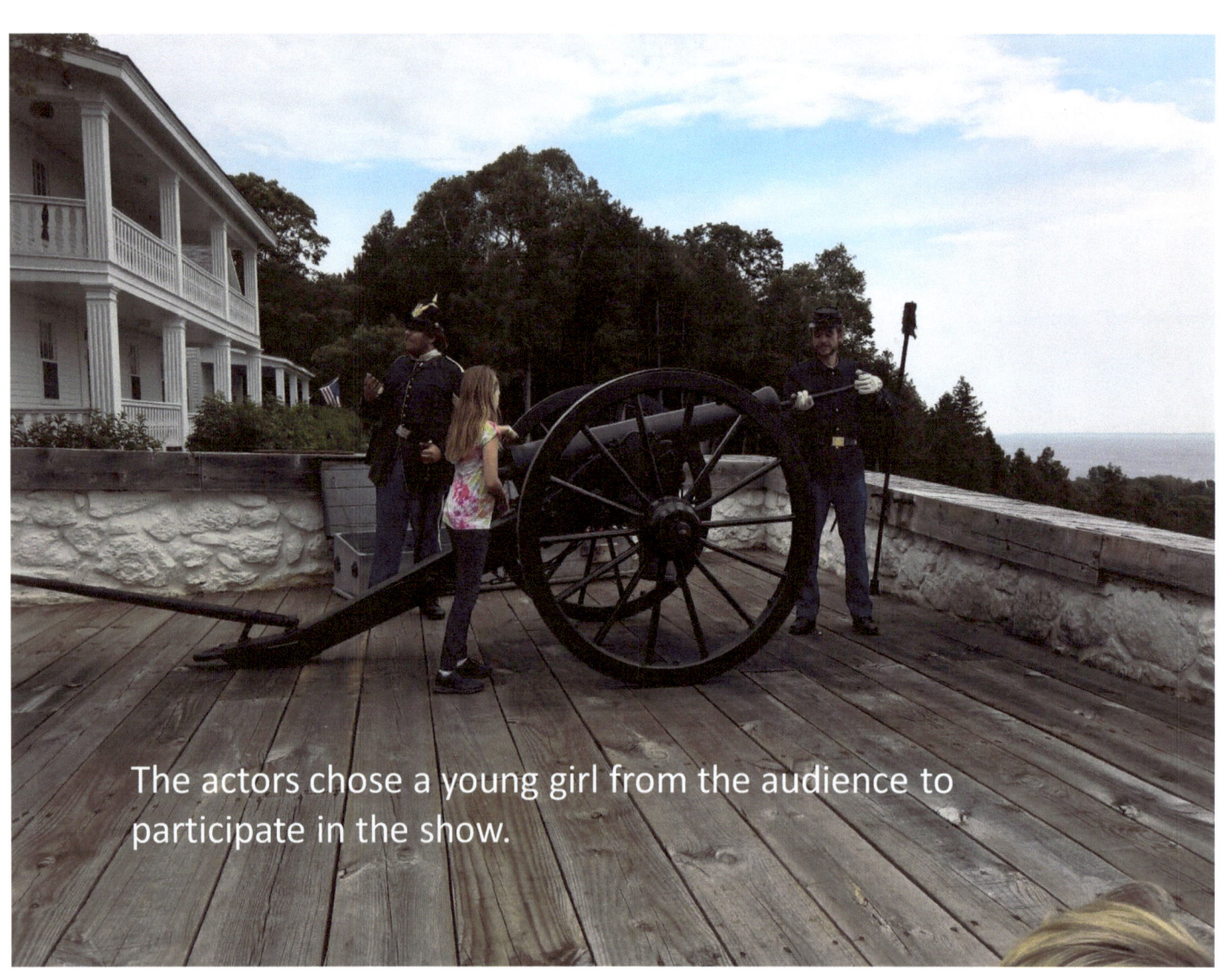

The actors chose a young girl from the audience to participate in the show.

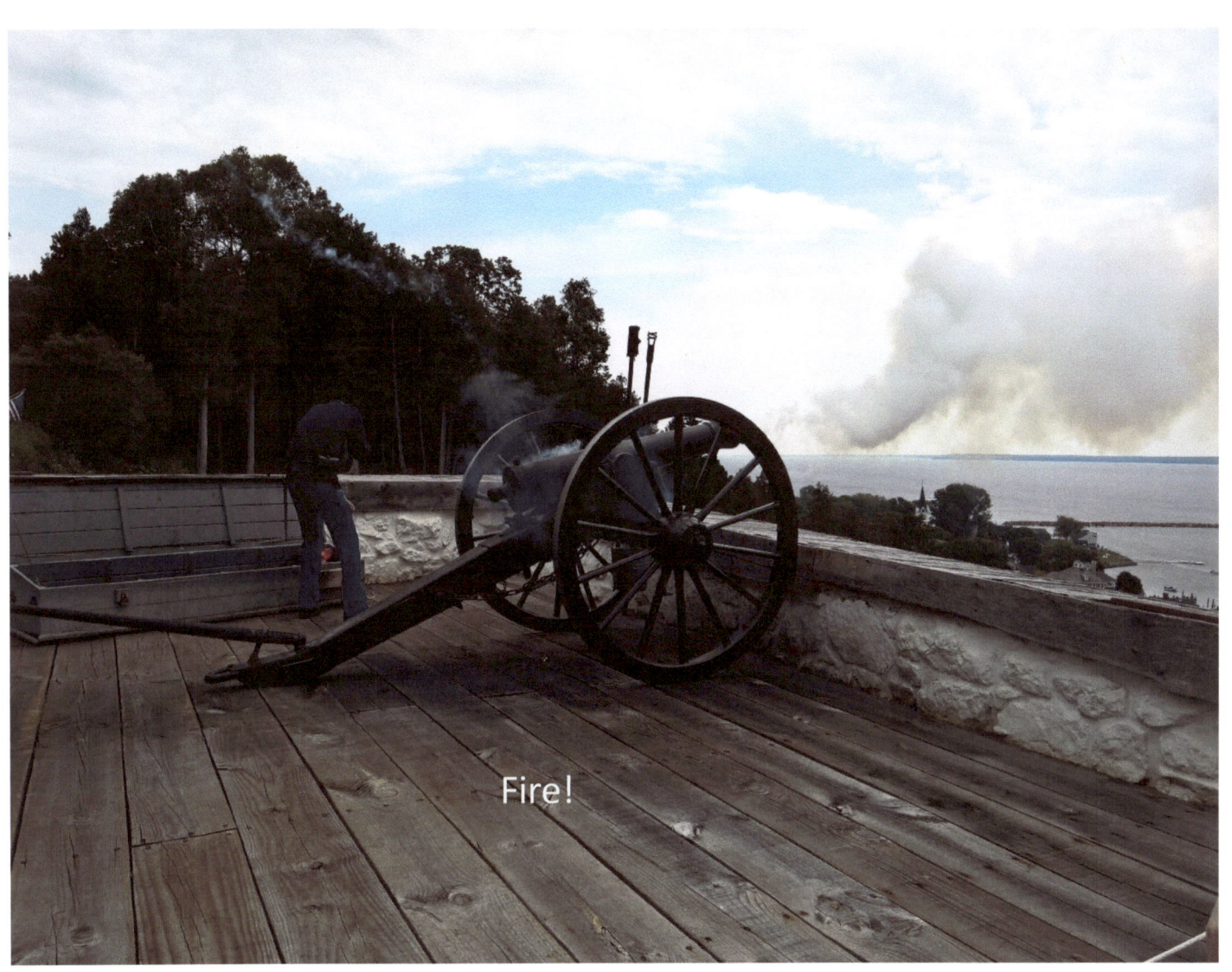

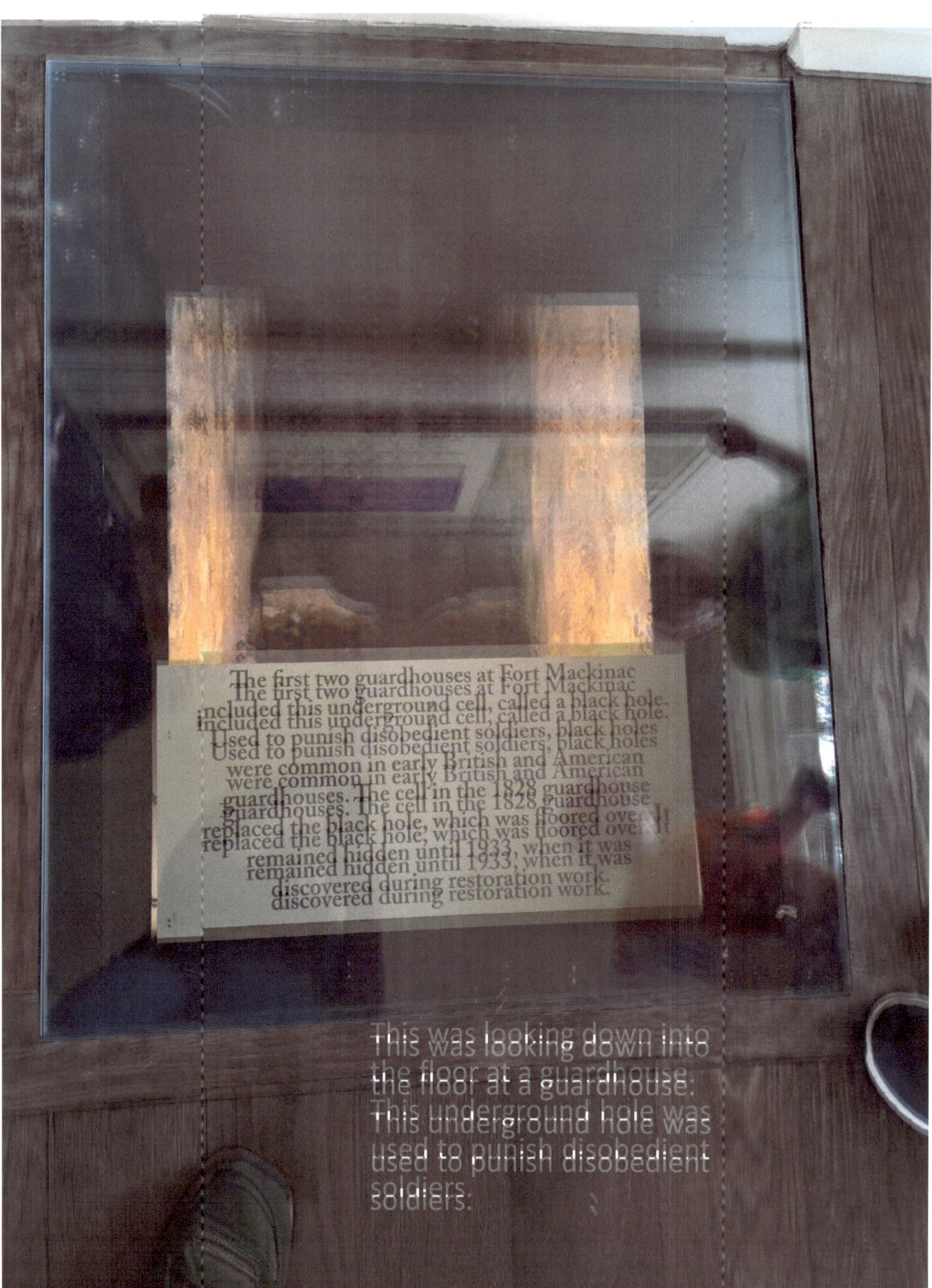

The first two guardhouses at Fort Mackinac included this underground cell, called a black hole. Used to punish disobedient soldiers, black holes were common in early British and American guardhouses. The cell in the 1828 guardhouse replaced the black hole, which was floored over. remained hidden until 1933, when it was discovered during restoration work.

This was looking down into the floor at a guardhouse. This underground hole was used to punish disobedient soldiers.

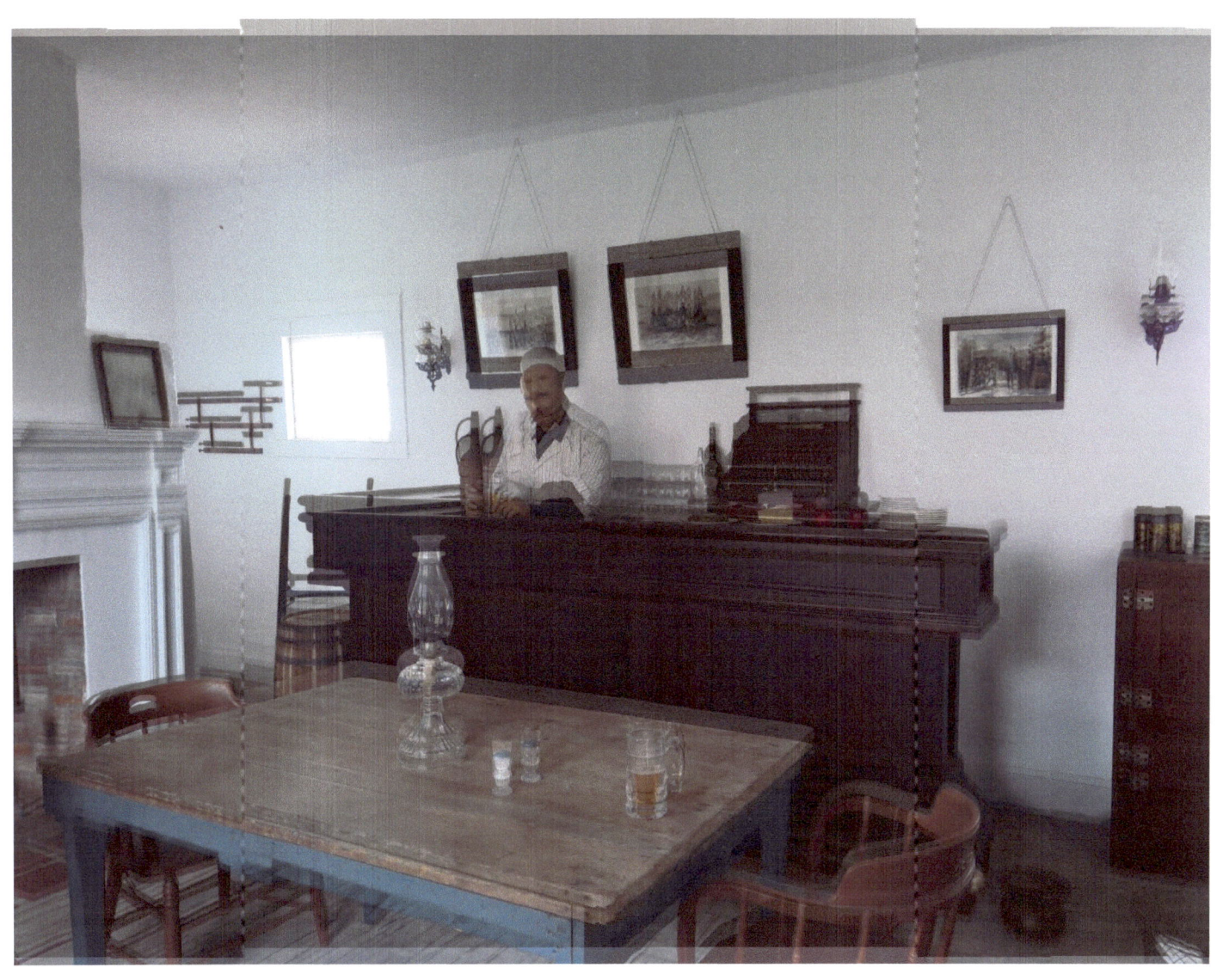

This was part of the old canteen in the fort. It has wonderful life-like wax figurines showcasing how the areas were used.

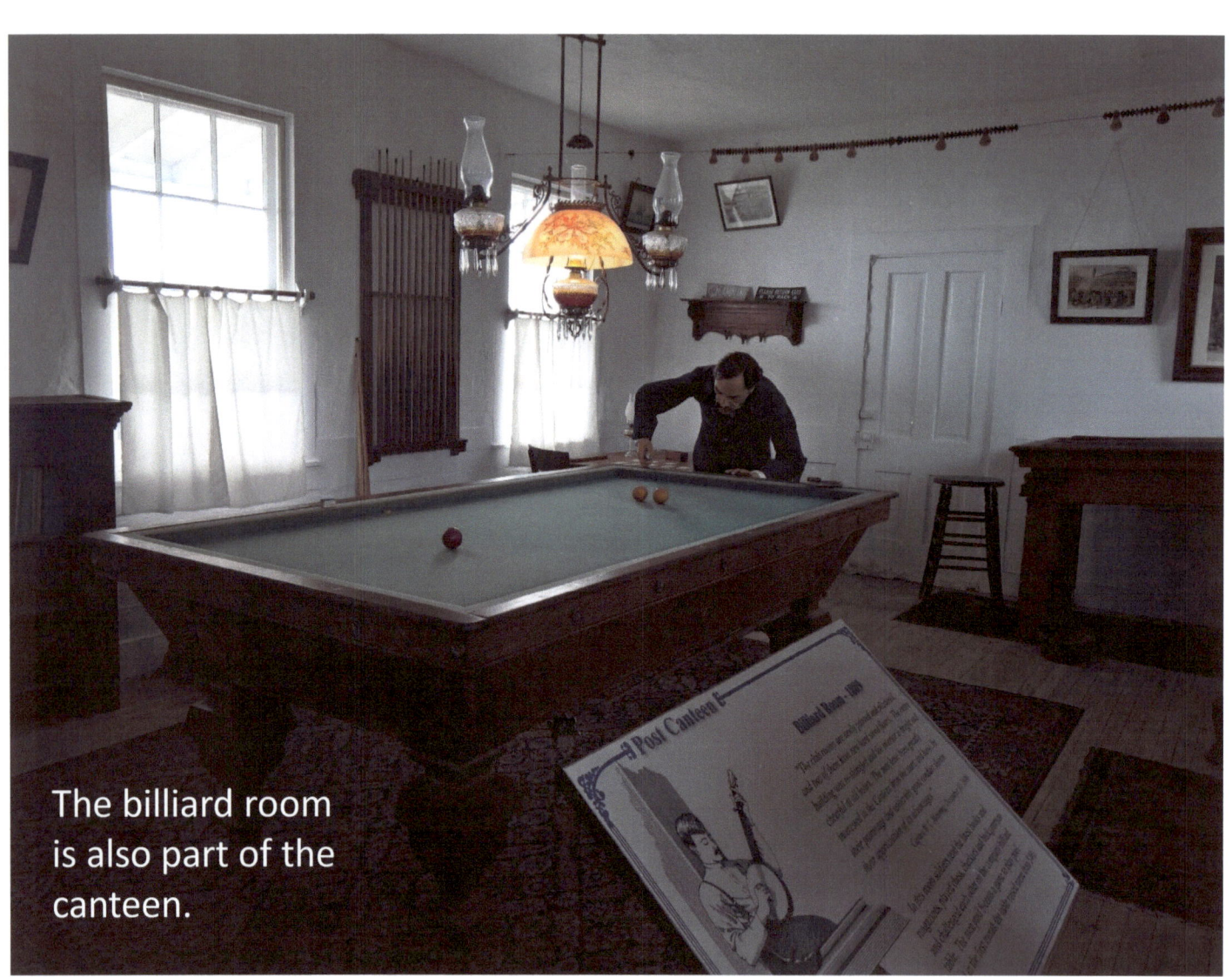

The billiard room is also part of the canteen.

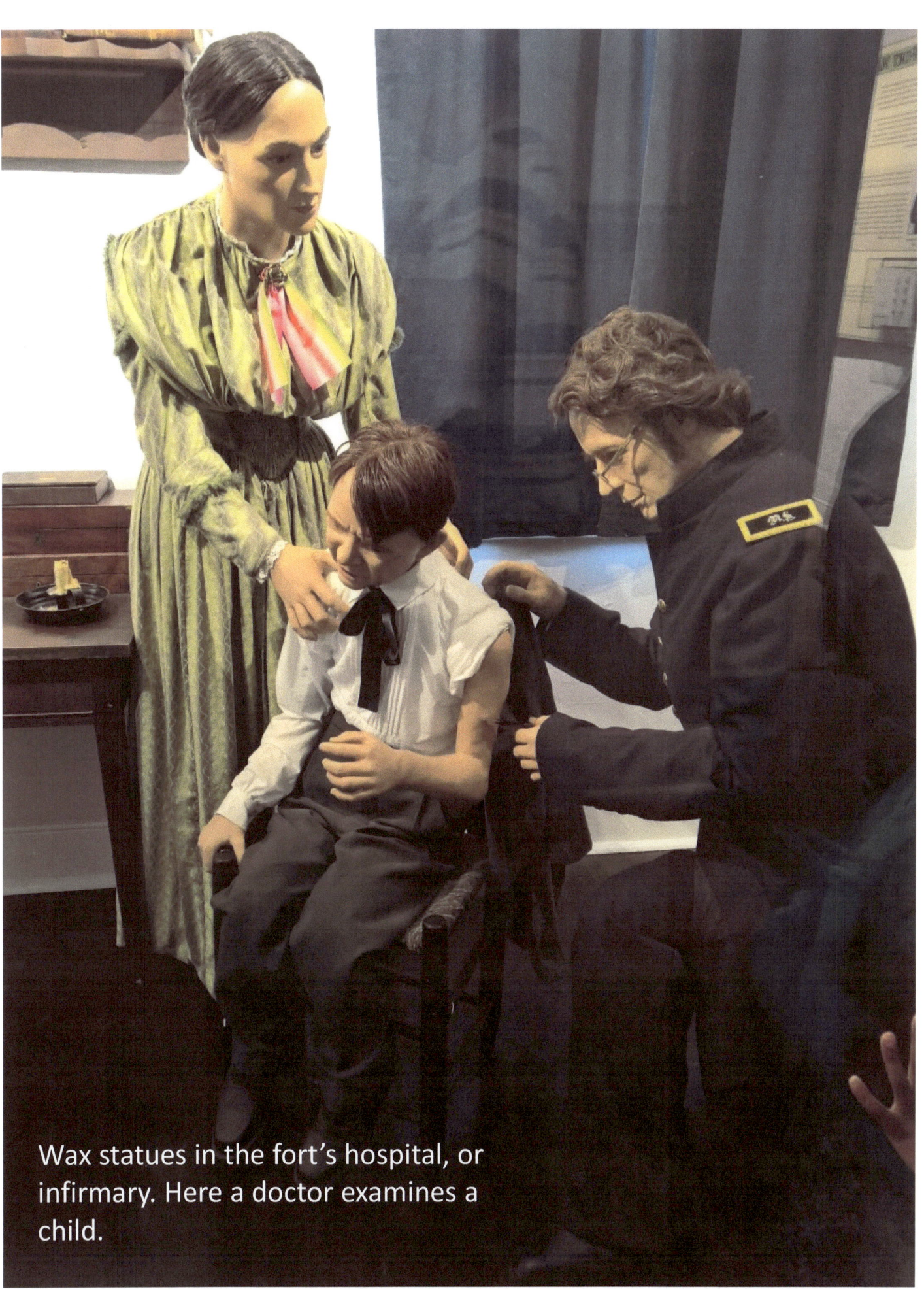

Wax statues in the fort's hospital, or infirmary. Here a doctor examines a child.

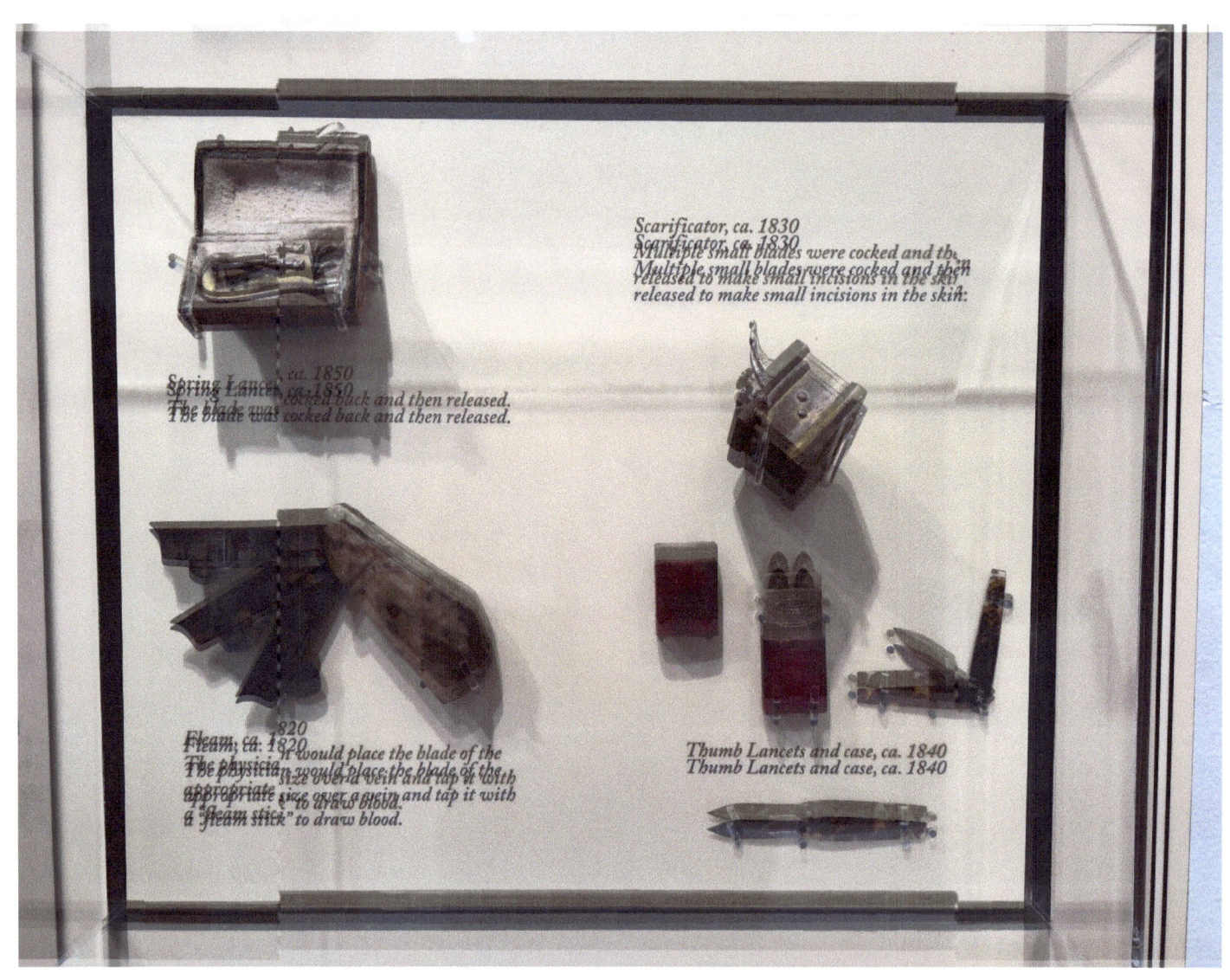

Examples of implements doctors used when treating patients.

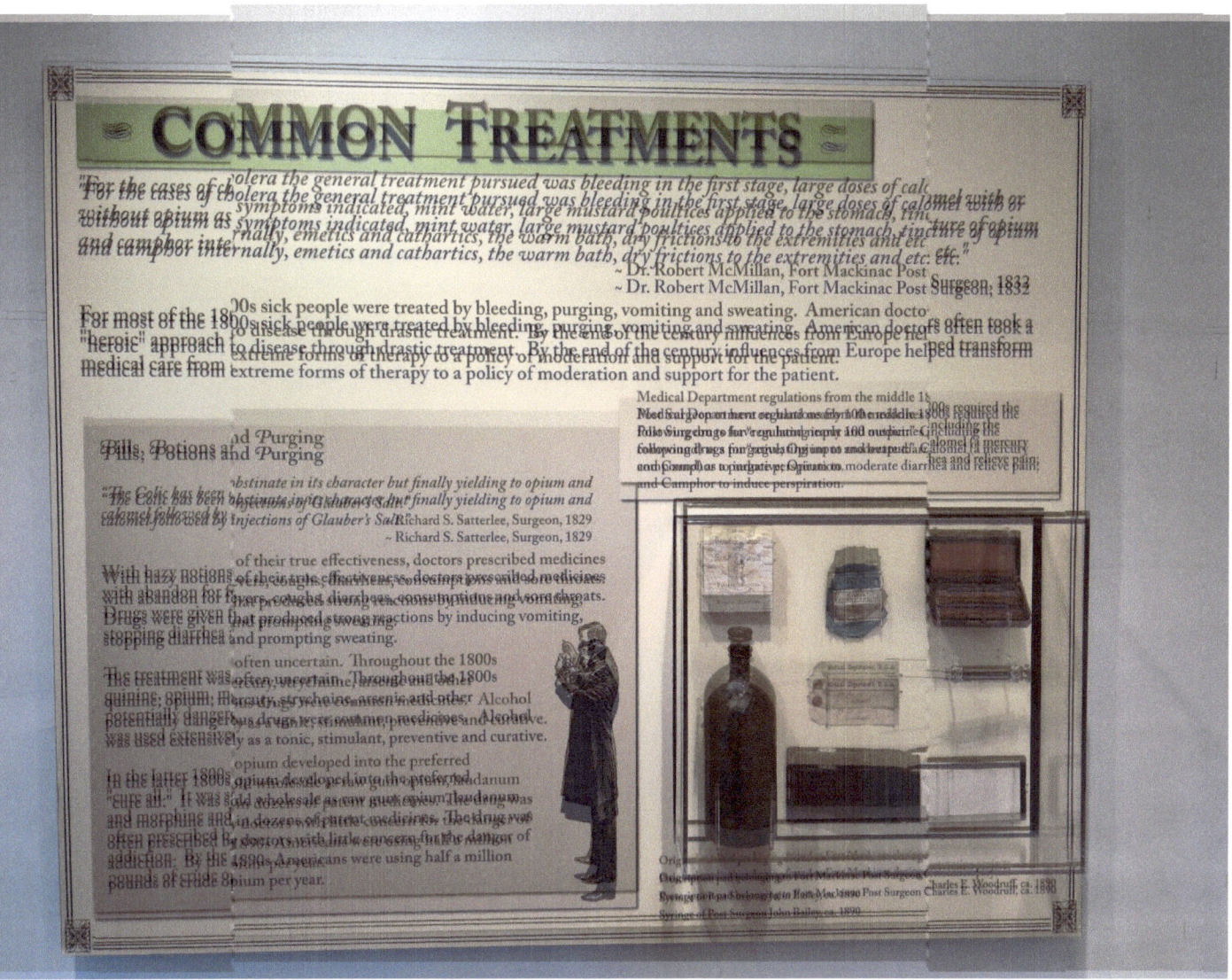

Common Treatments

"For the cases of cholera the general treatment pursued was bleeding in the first stage, large doses of calomel with or without opium as symptoms indicated, mint water, large mustard poultices applied to the stomach, tincture of opium and camphor internally, emetics and cathartics, the warm bath, dry frictions to the extremities and etc. etc."
~ Dr. Robert McMillan, Fort Mackinac Post Surgeon, 1833

For most of the 1800s sick people were treated by bleeding, purging, vomiting and sweating. American doctors often took a "heroic" approach to disease through drastic treatment. By the end of the century influences from Europe helped transform medical care from extreme forms of therapy to a policy of moderation and support for the patient.

Pills, Potions and Purging

"The Colic has been obstinate in its character but finally yielding to opium and calomel followed by Injections of Glauber's Sal..."
~ Richard S. Satterlee, Surgeon, 1829

With hazy notions of their true effectiveness, doctors prescribed medicines with abandon for fevers, coughs, diarrhea, consumption and sore throats. Drugs were given that produced strong reactions by inducing vomiting, stopping diarrhea and prompting sweating.

The treatment was often uncertain. Throughout the 1800s quinine, opium, mercury, strychnine, arsenic and other potentially dangerous drugs were common medicines. Alcohol was used extensively as a tonic, stimulant, preventive and curative.

In the latter 1800s opium developed into the preferred "cure all." It was sold wholesale as raw gum opium, laudanum and morphine and in dozens of patent medicines. The drug was often prescribed by doctors with little concern for the danger of addiction. By the 1890s Americans were using half a million pounds of crude opium per year.

Medical Department regulations from the middle 1800s required the following drugs for regular supply to military posts including: Calomel (a mercury compound) as a purgative, Opium to moderate diarrhea and relieve pain, and Camphor to induce perspiration.

Original opium pad belonging to Fort Mackinac Post Surgeon Charles E. Woodruff, ca. 1890
Syringe of Post Surgeon John Bailey, ca. 1870

The infirmary/hospital has a lot of information about how diseases and injuries were handled in the early 1800s.

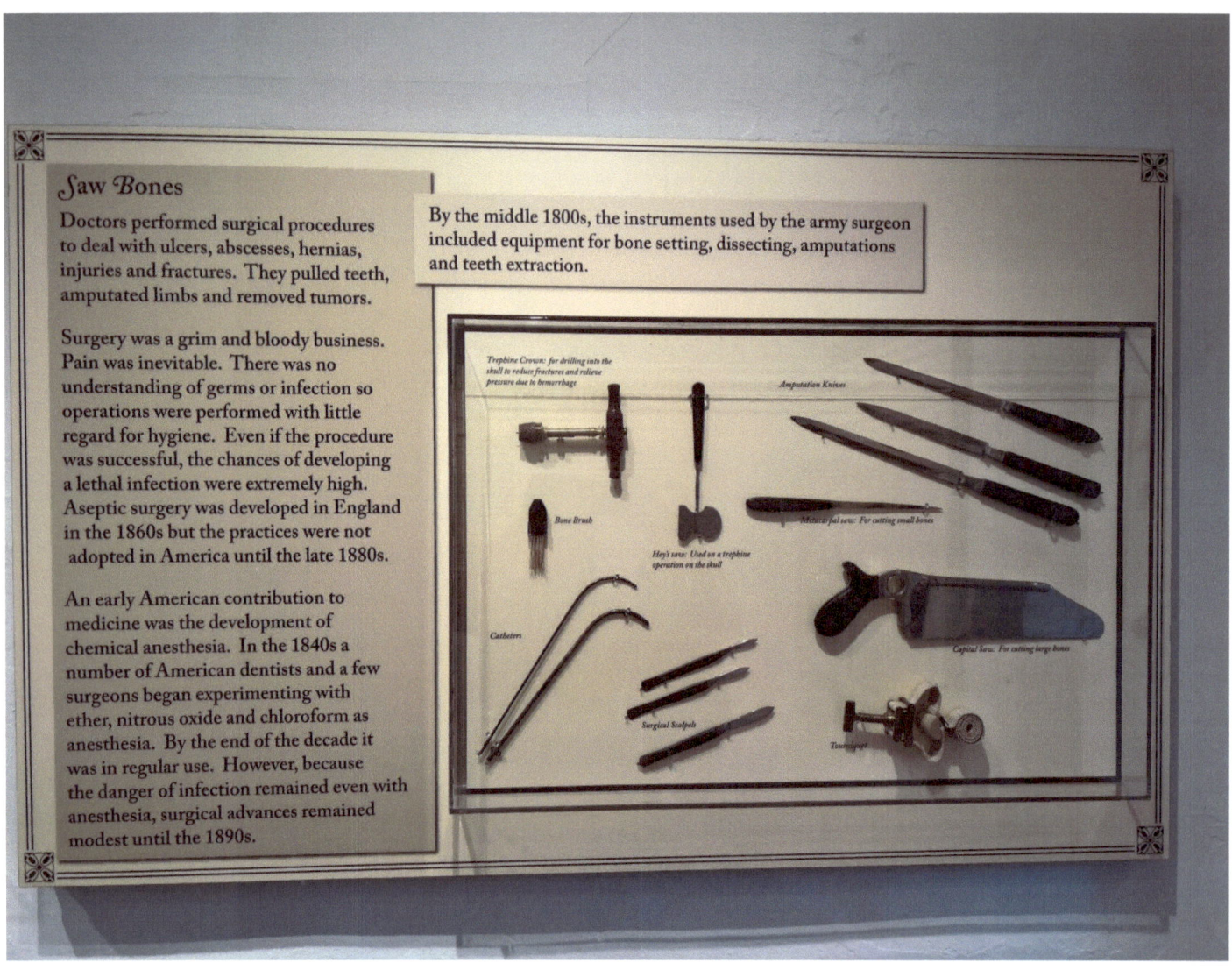

More primitive surgical tools, with explanations as to how they were used.

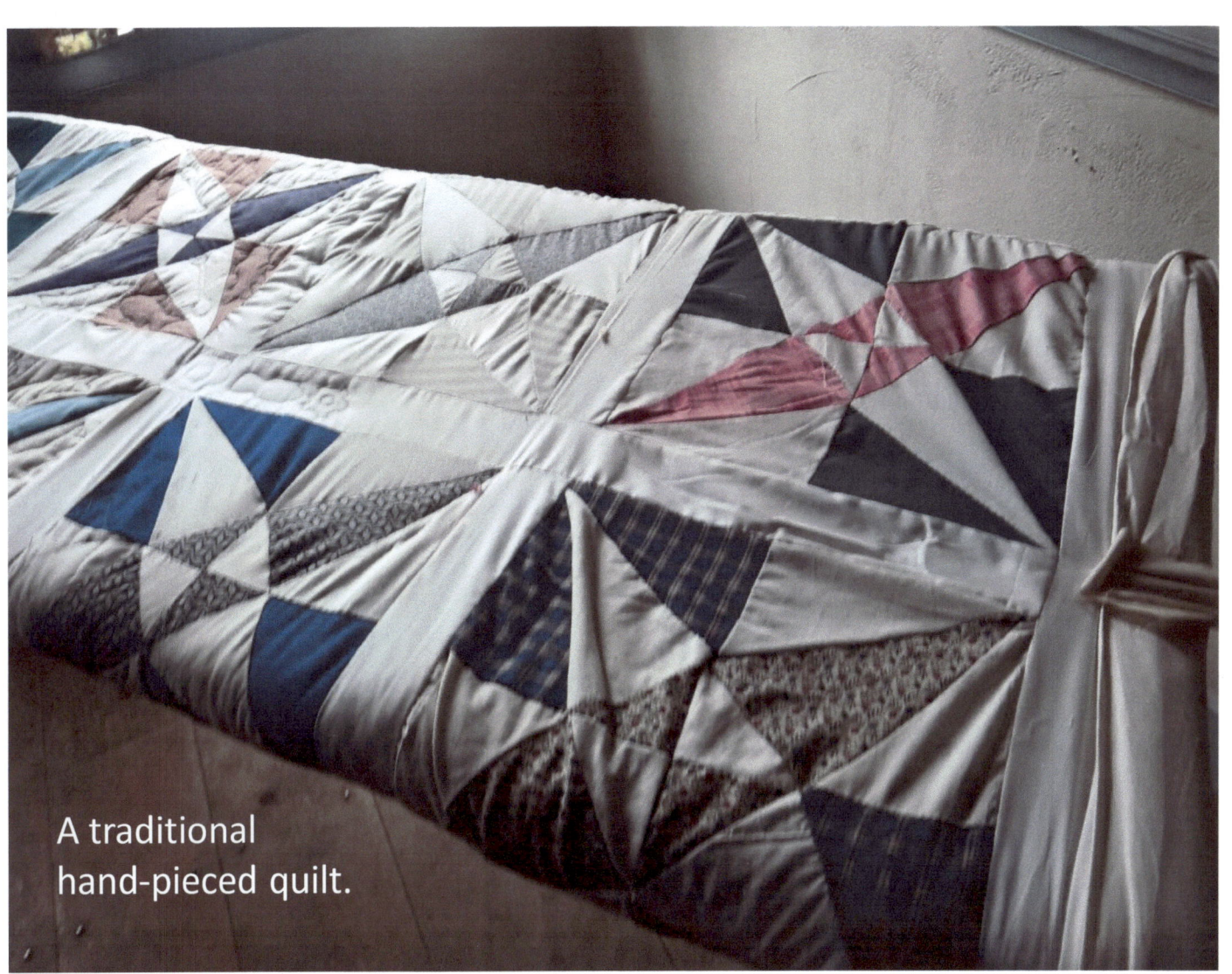

A traditional hand-pieced quilt.

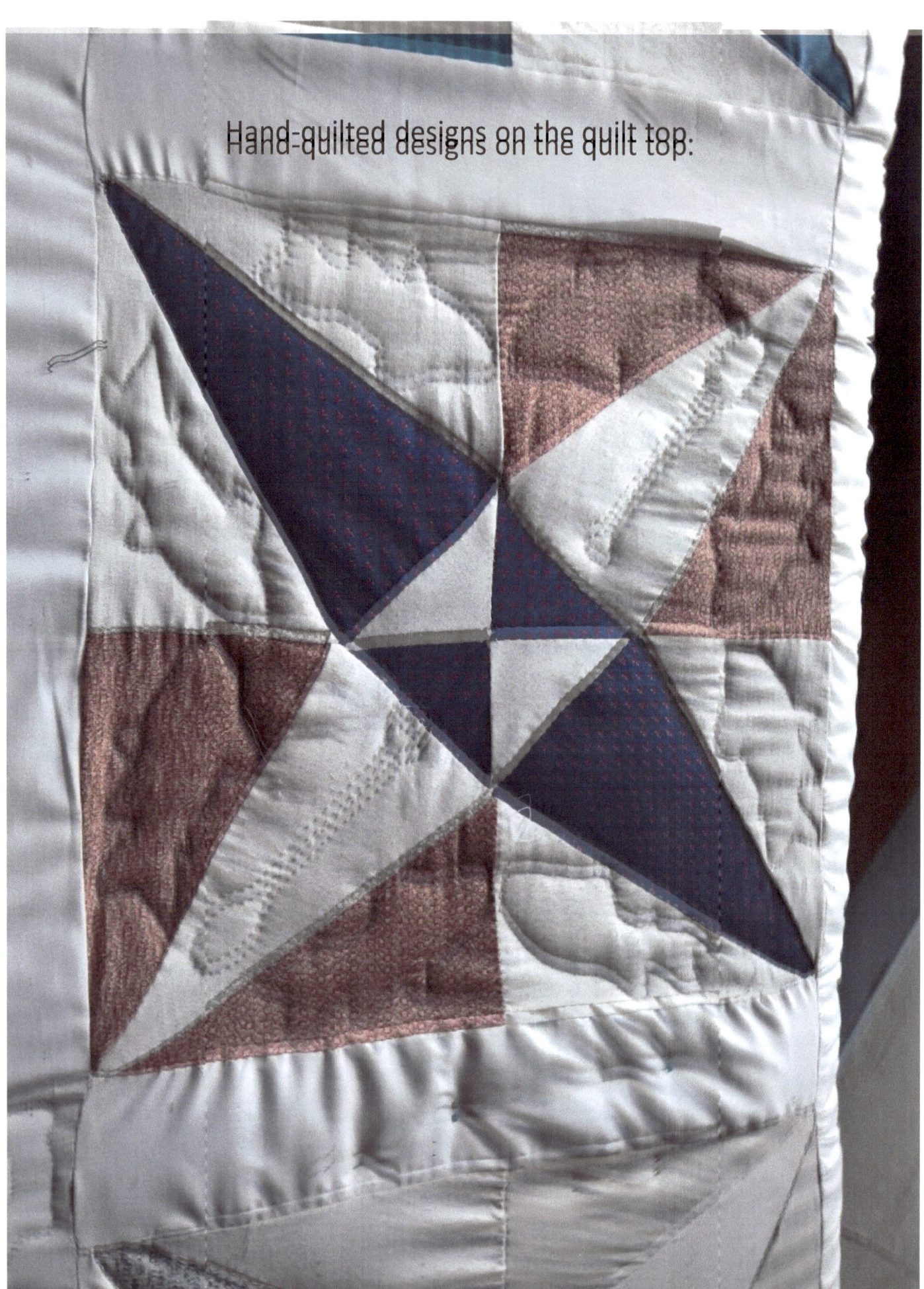

Hand-quilted designs on the quilt top:

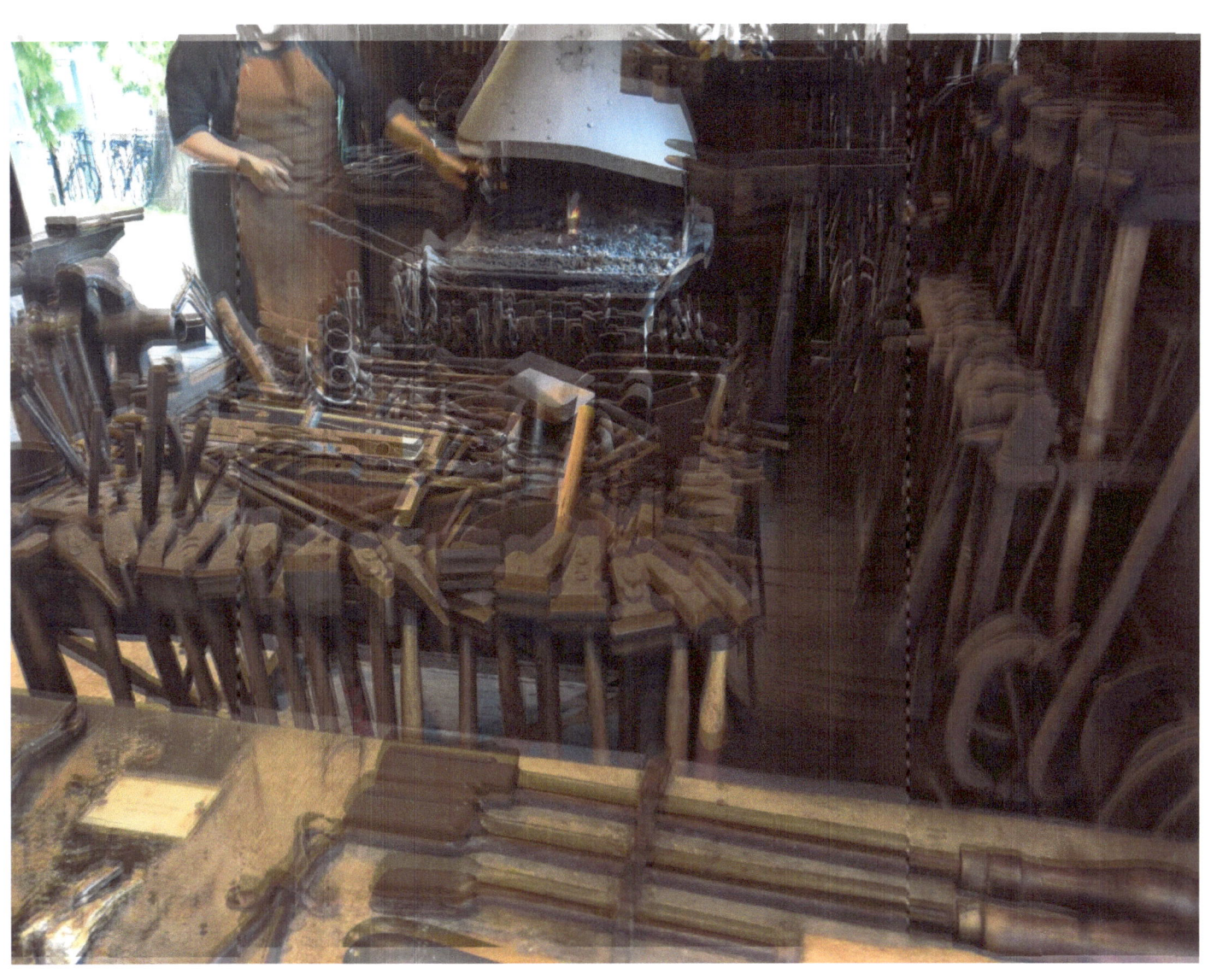

An operational blacksmith shop is filled with many types of hand-forged tools.

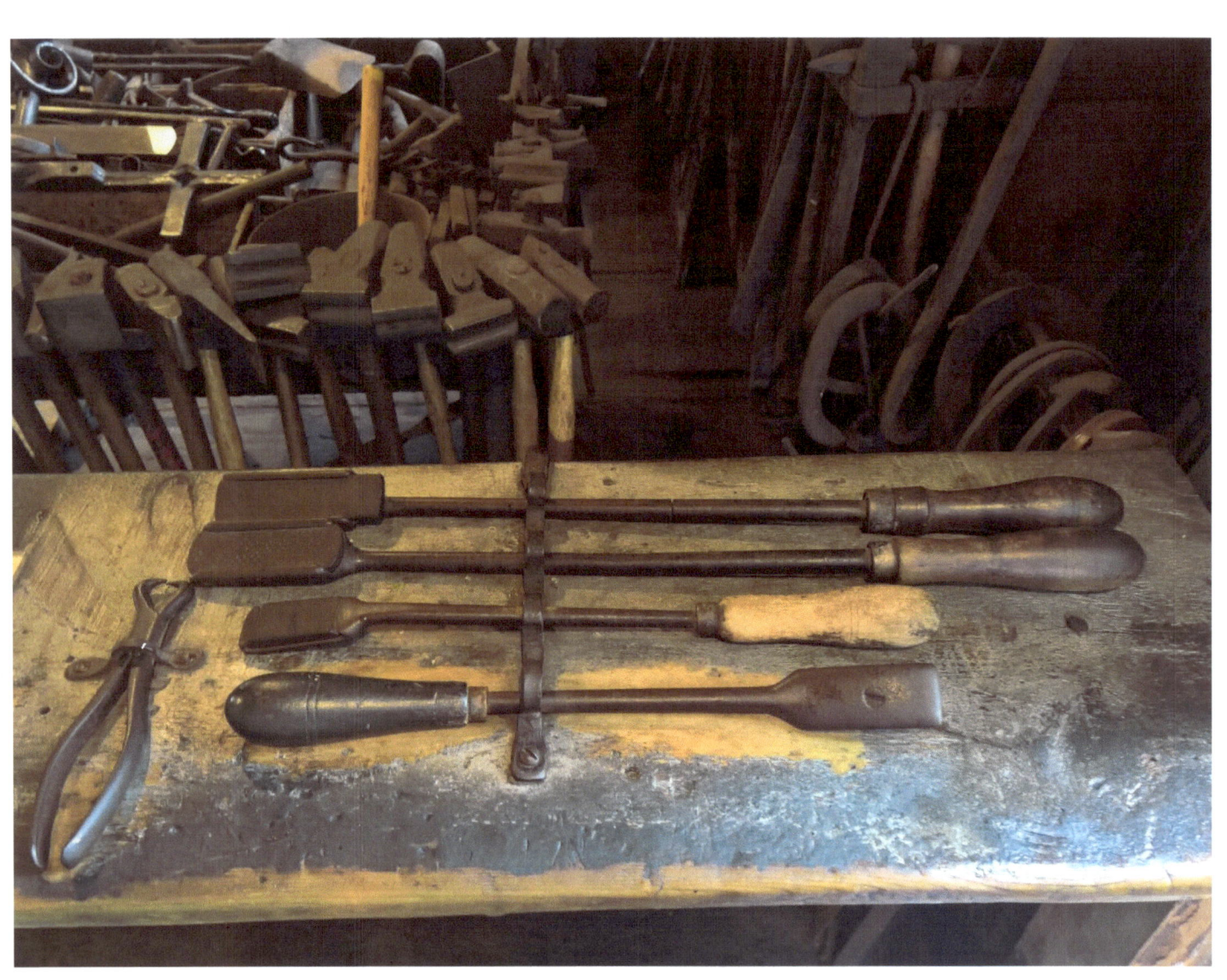

More tools in the blacksmith's shop.

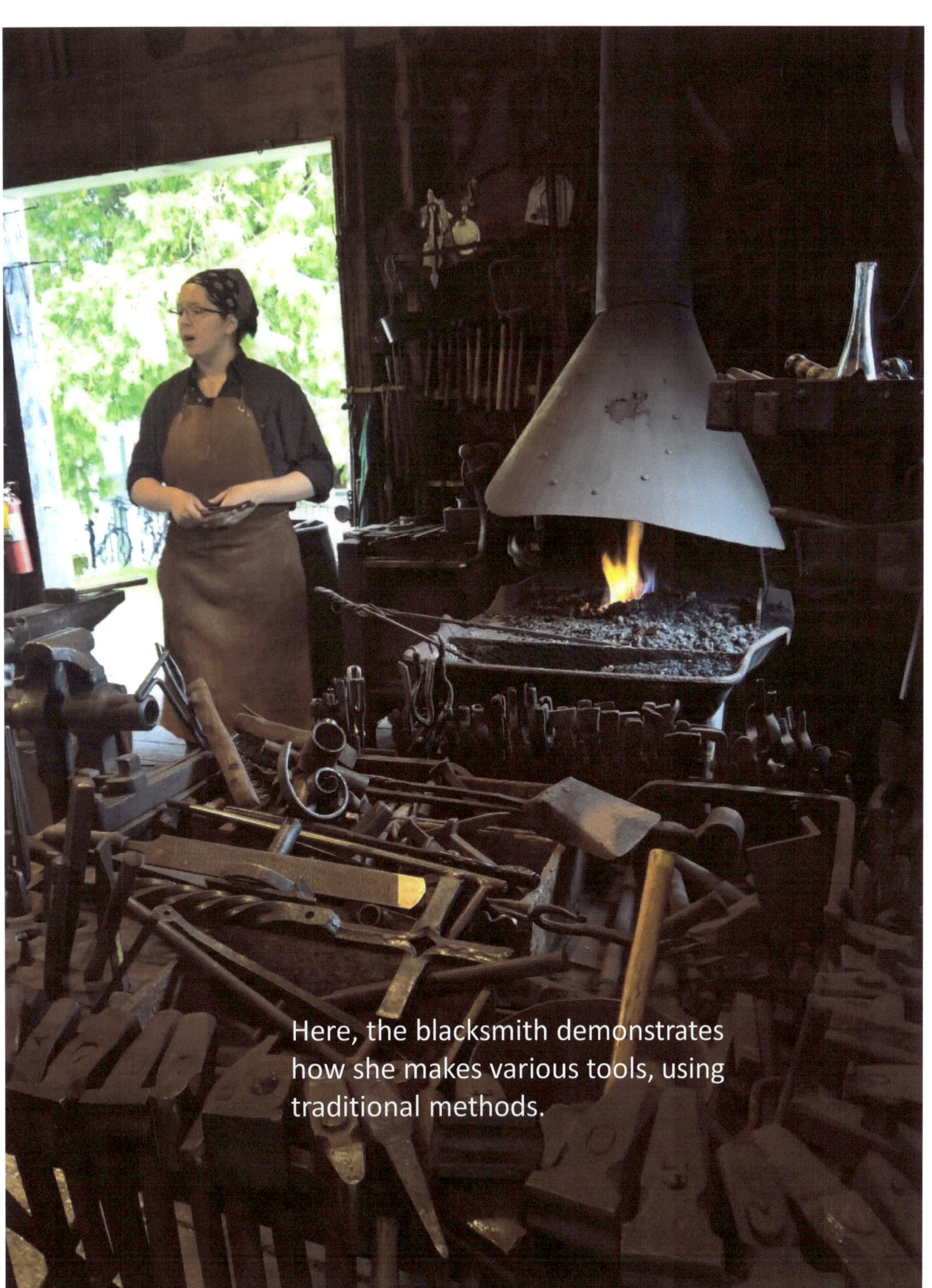

Here, the blacksmith demonstrates how she makes various tools, using traditional methods.

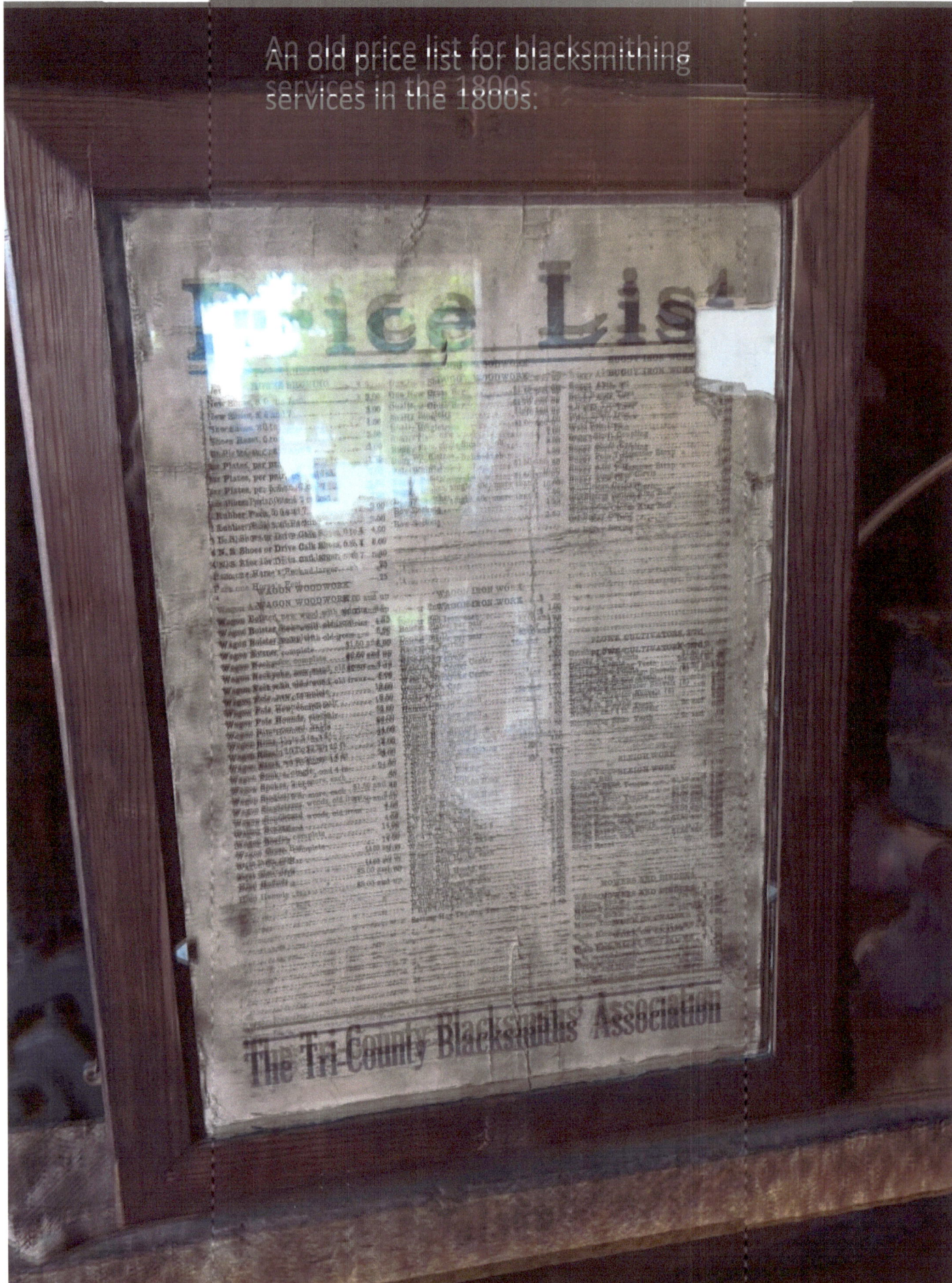

An old price list for blacksmithing services in the 1800s.

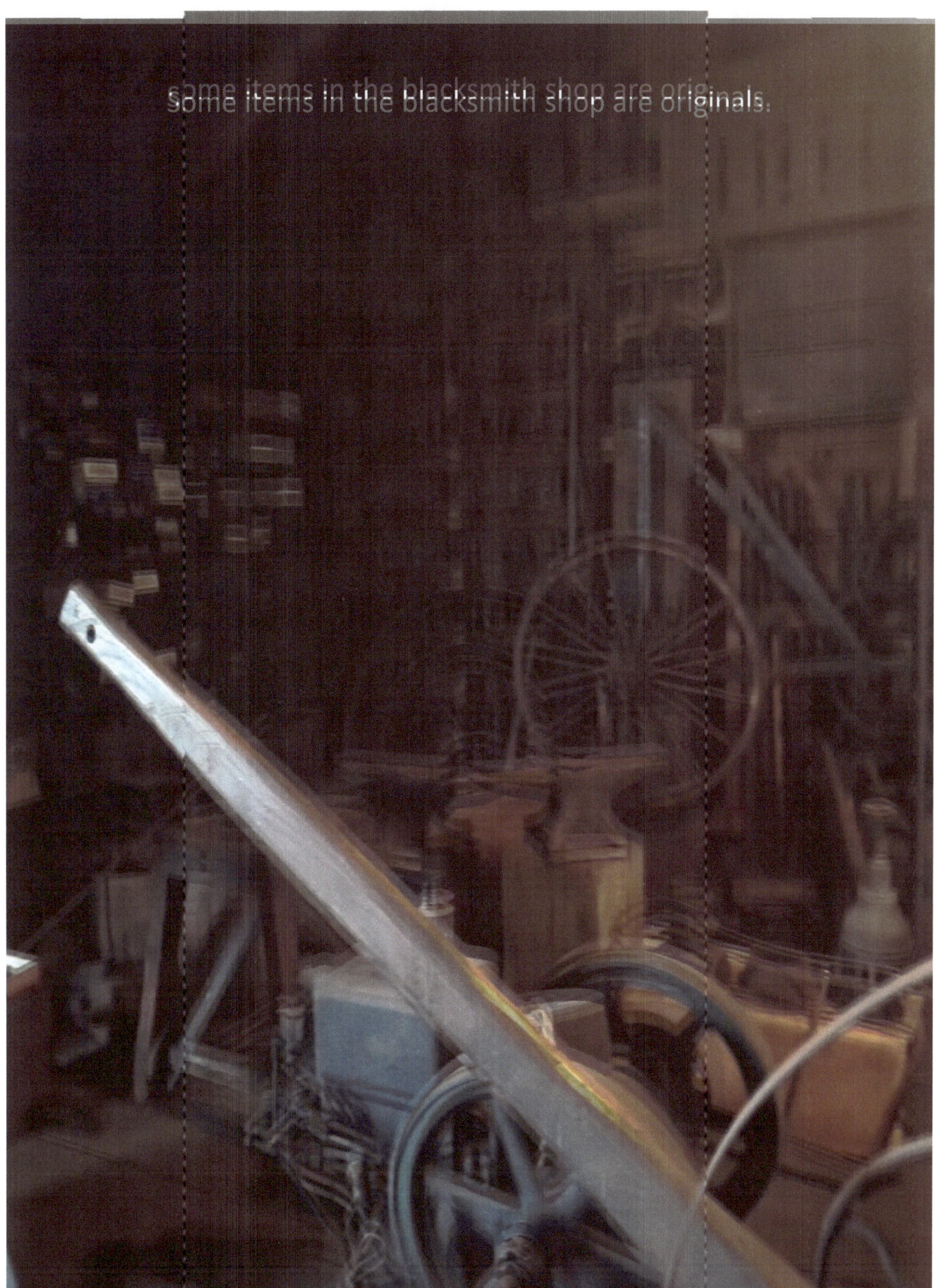
Some items in the blacksmith shop are originals.

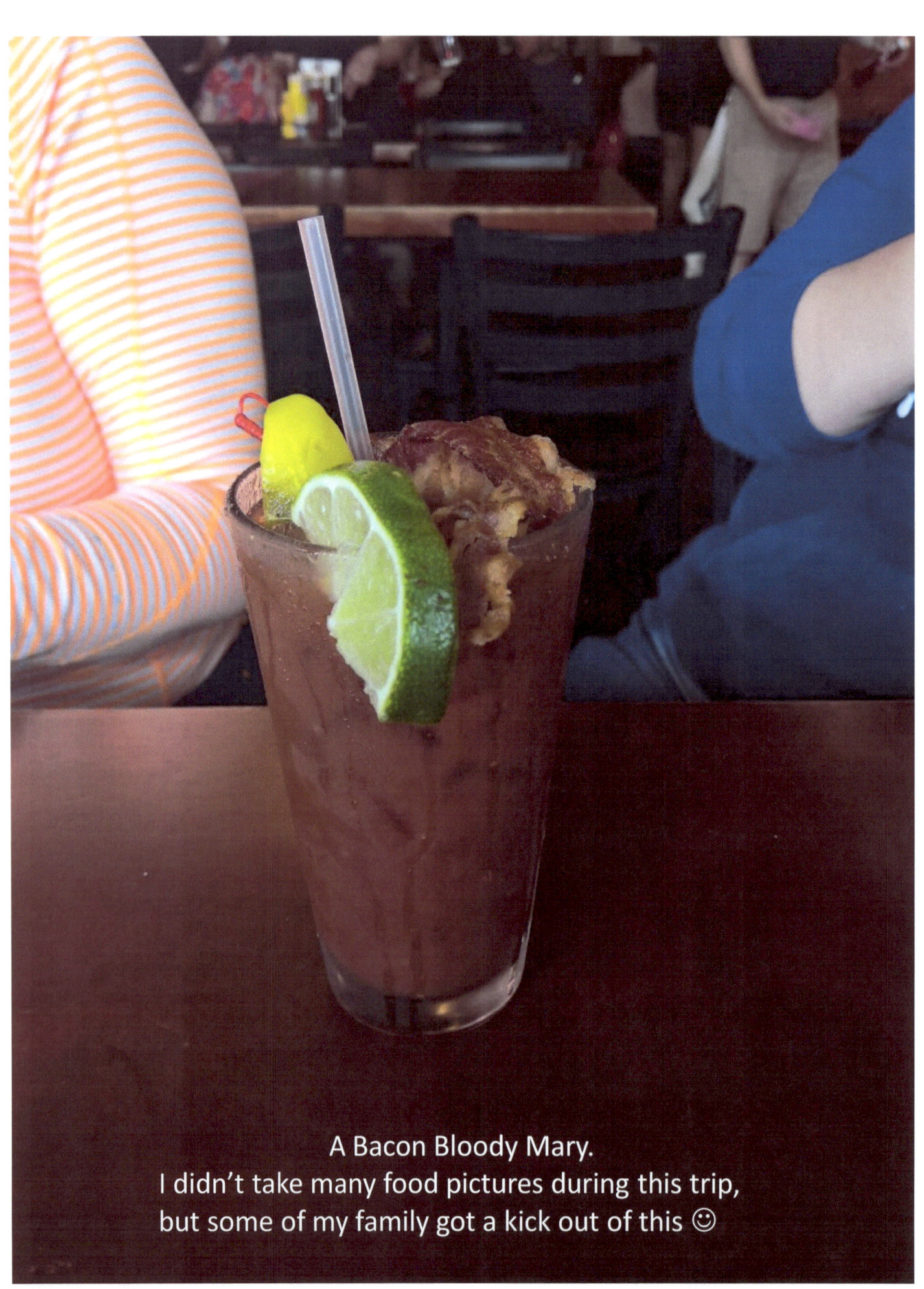

A Bacon Bloody Mary.
I didn't take many food pictures during this trip, but some of my family got a kick out of this ☺

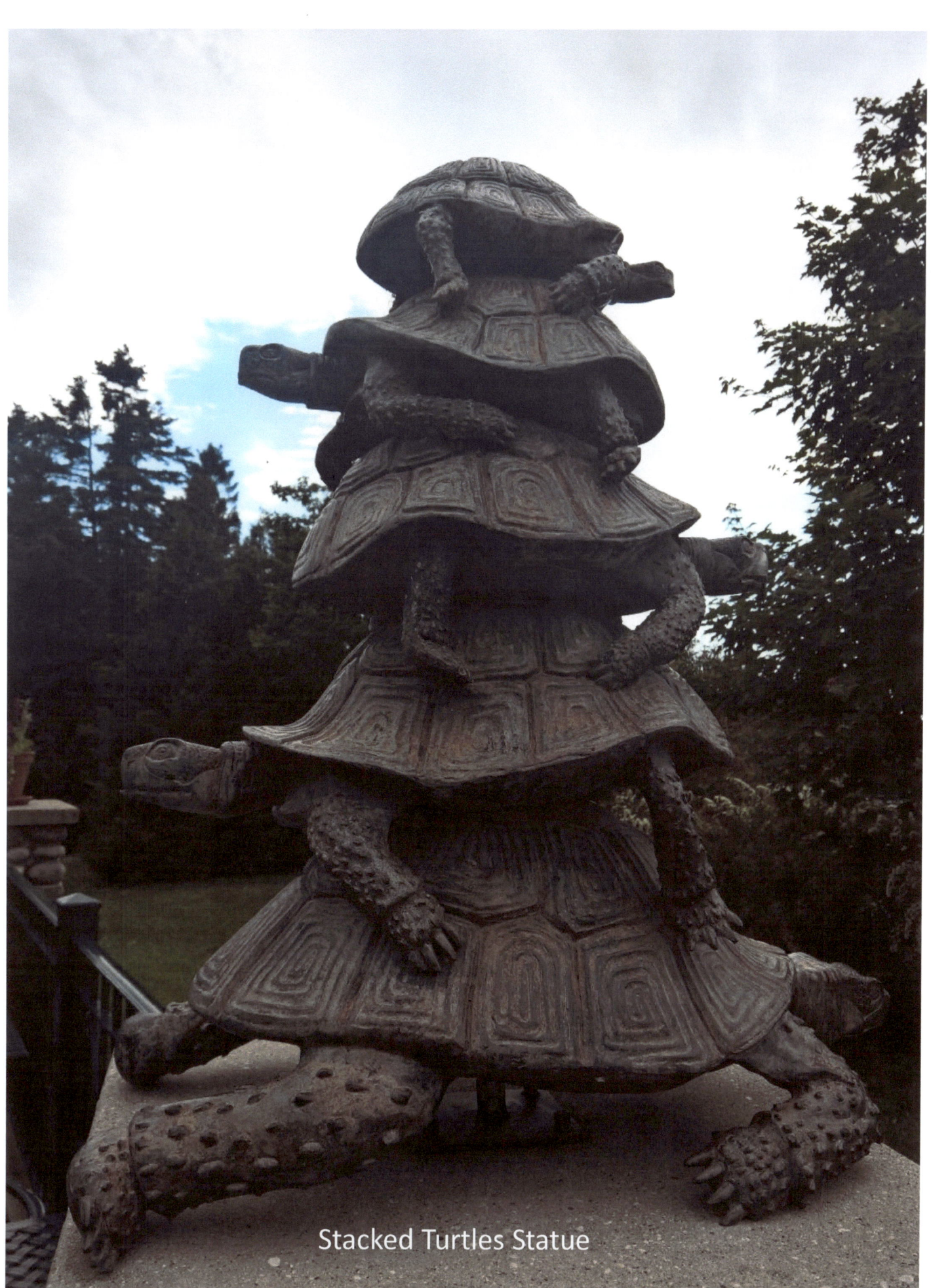
Stacked Turtles Statue

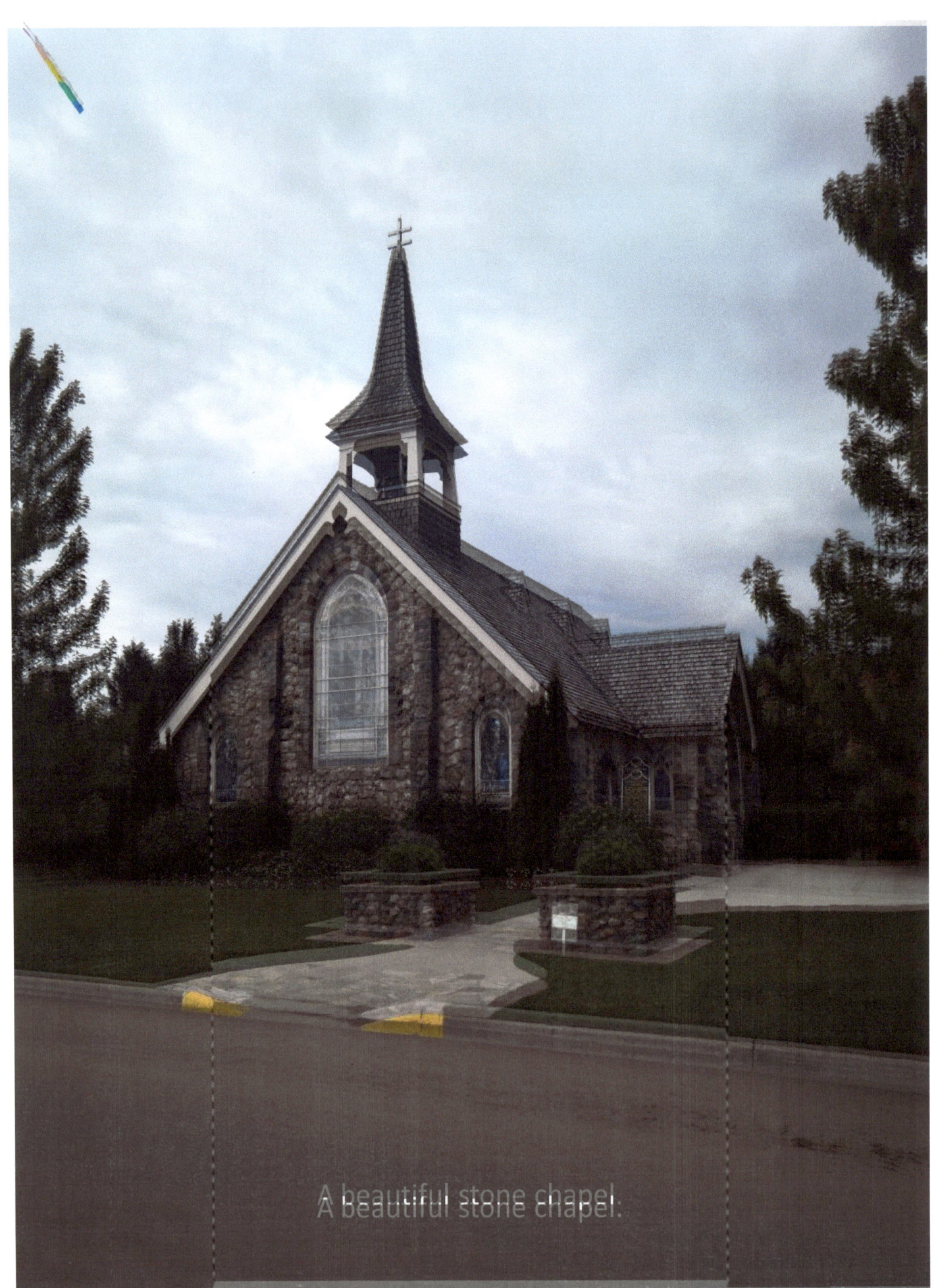

A beautiful stone chapel.

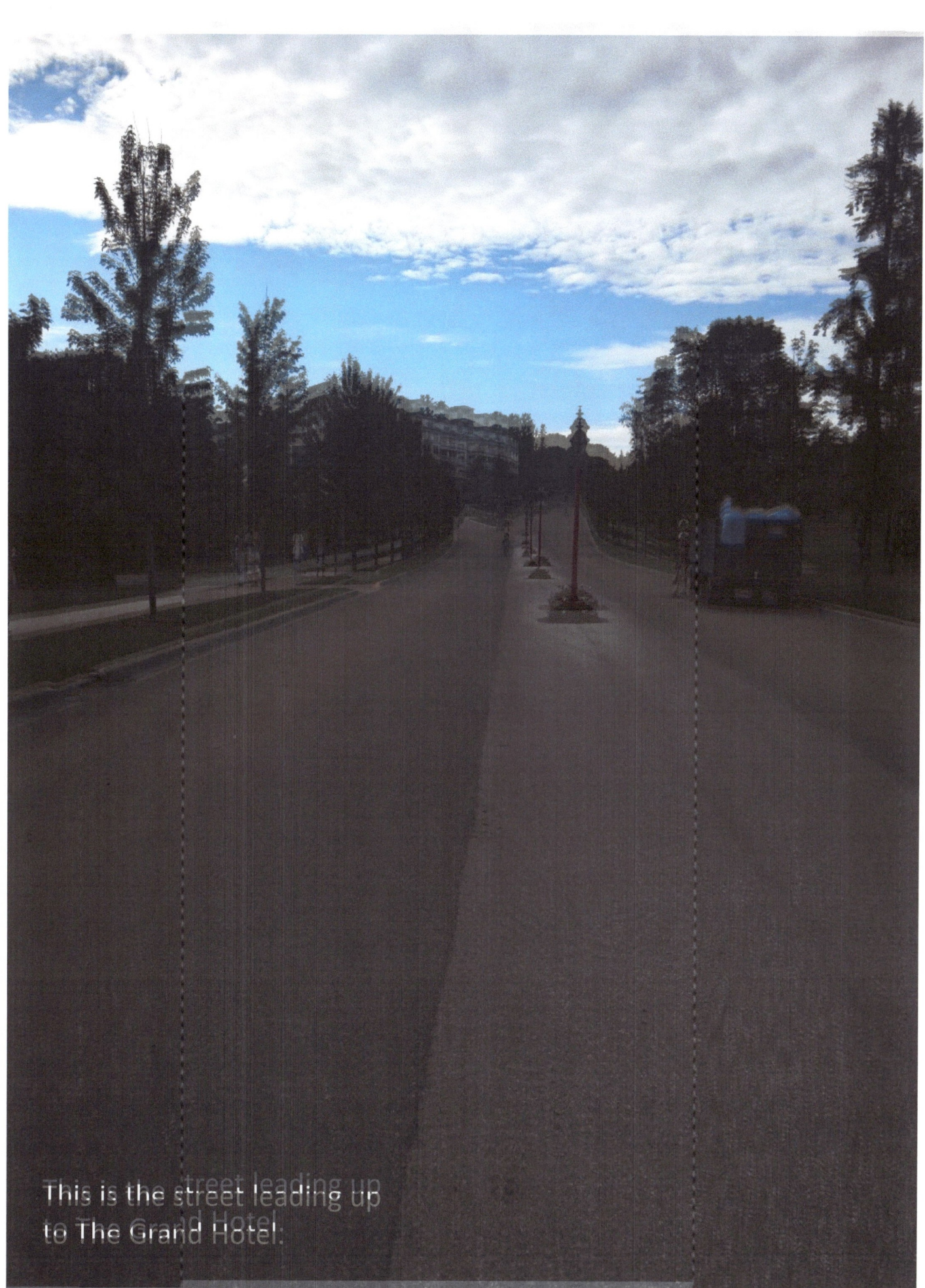

This is the street leading up to The Grand Hotel.

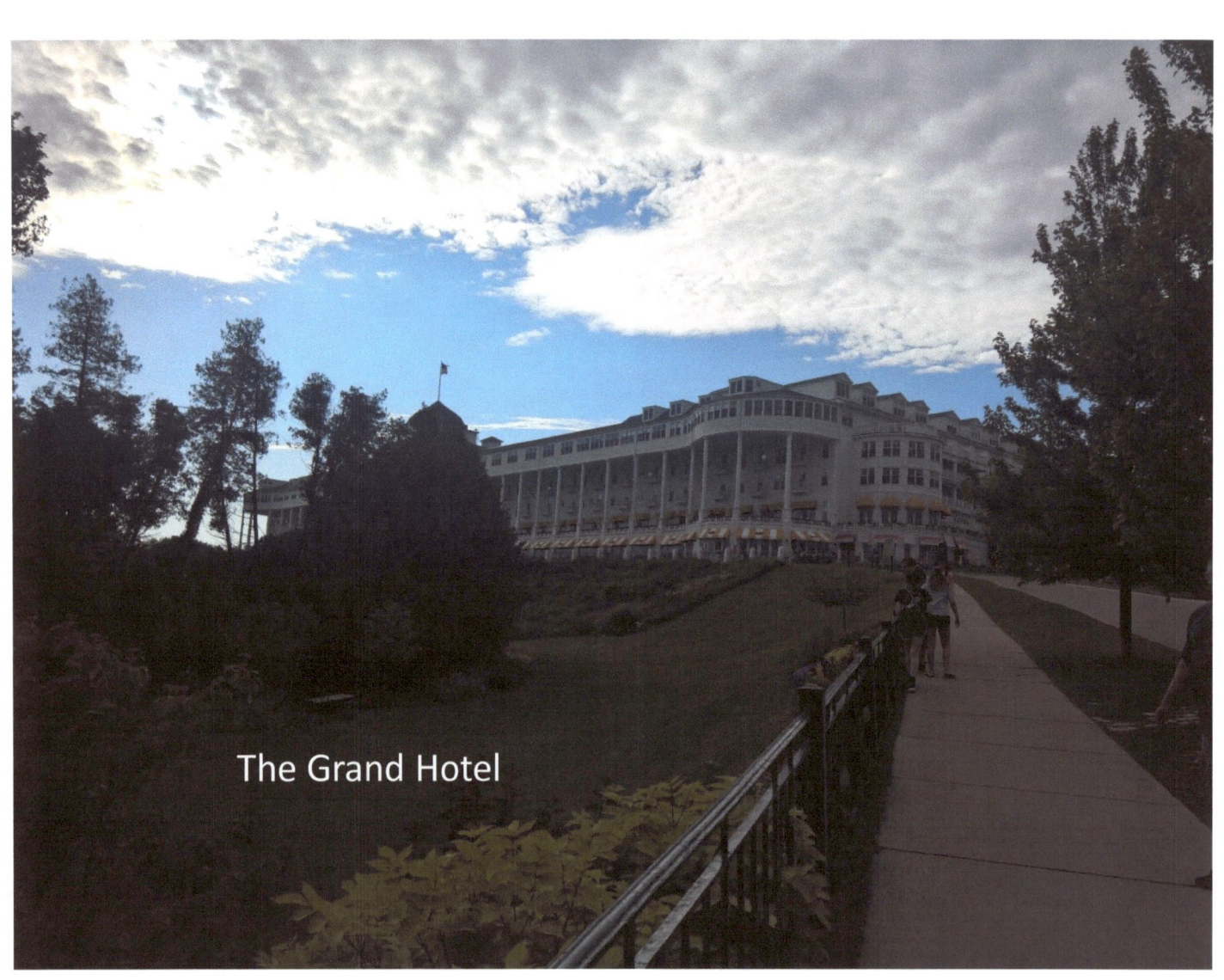
The Grand Hotel

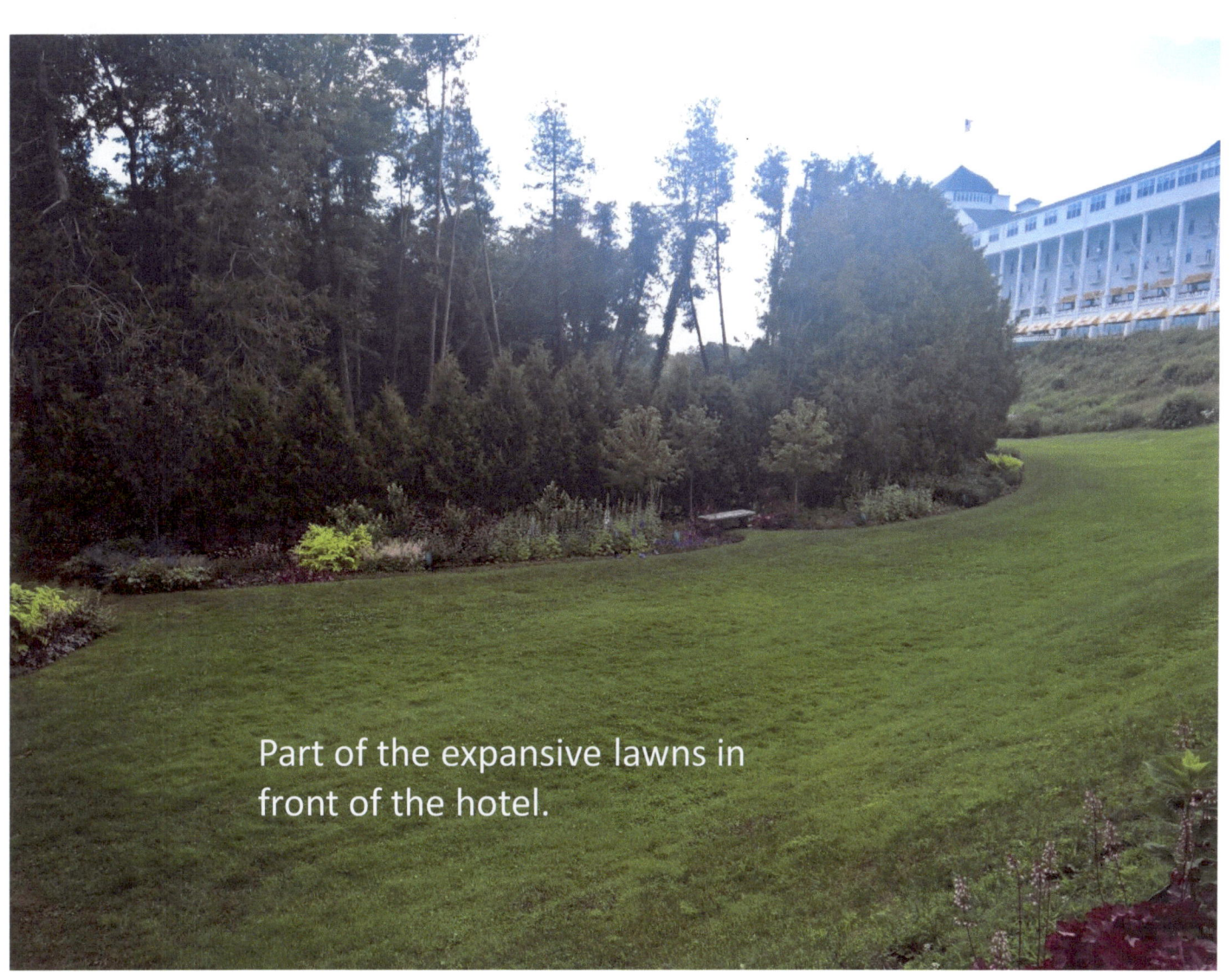
Part of the expansive lawns in front of the hotel.

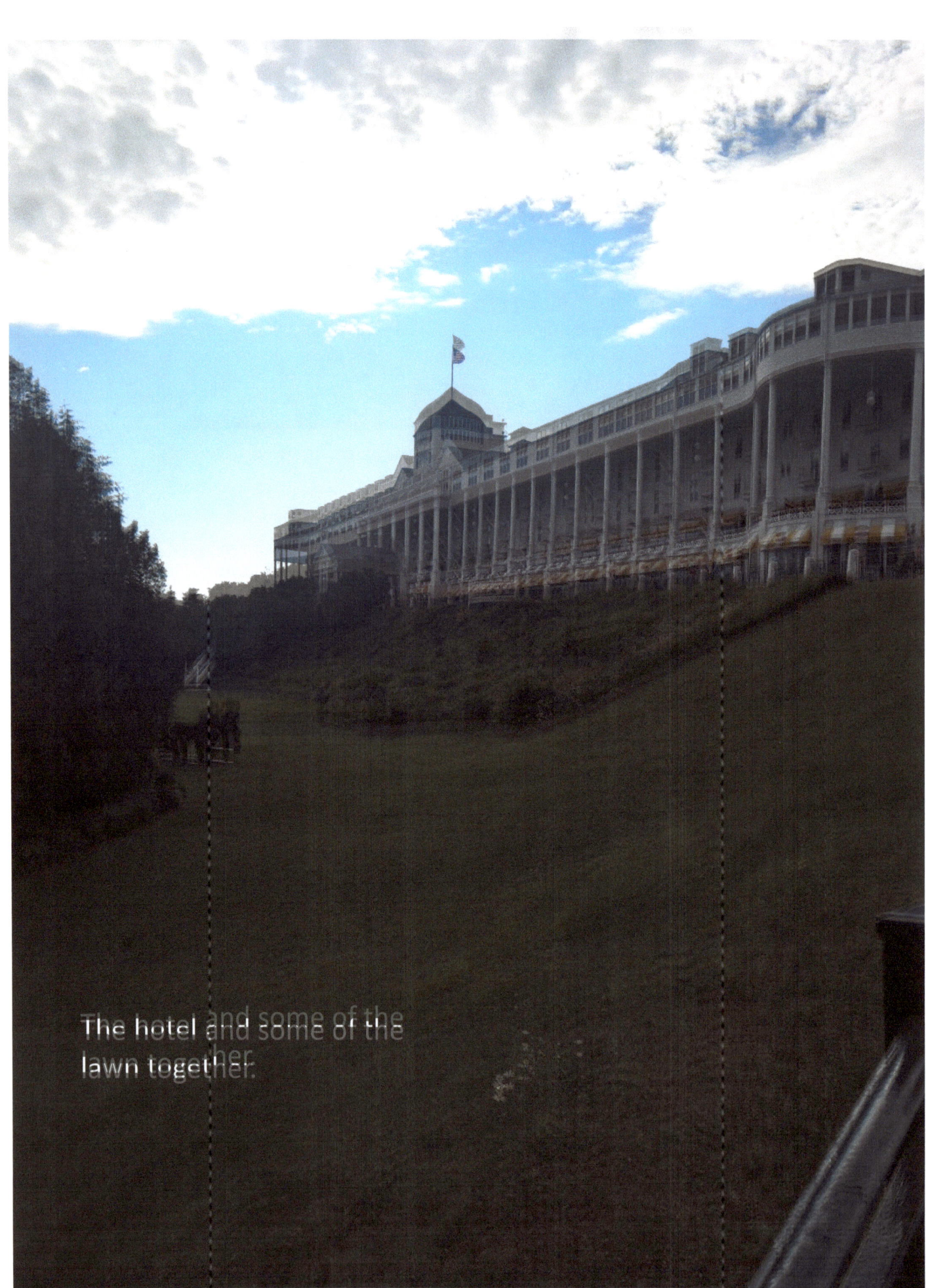

The hotel and some of the lawn together.

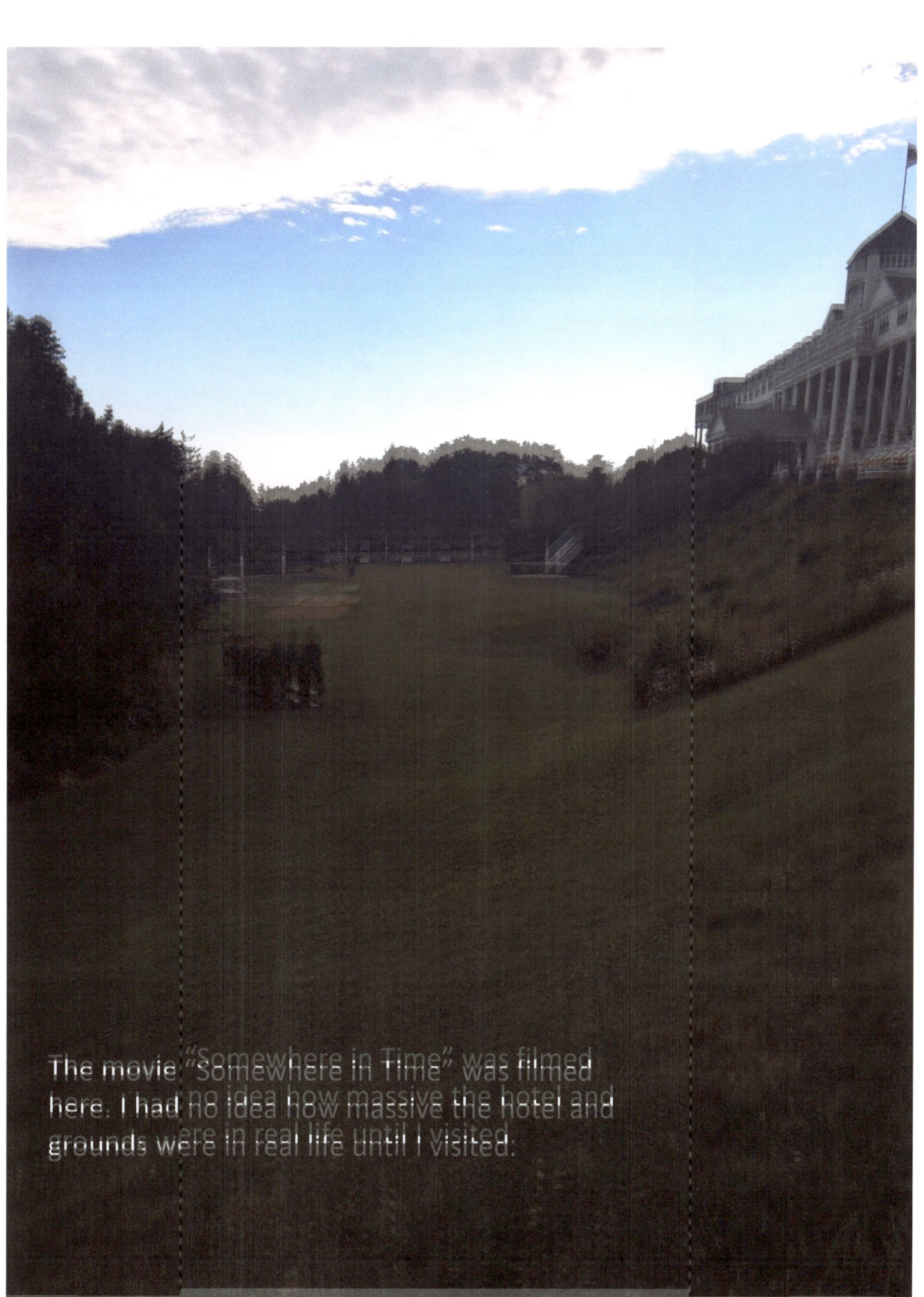
The movie "Somewhere in Time" was filmed here. I had no idea how massive the hotel and grounds were in real life until I visited.

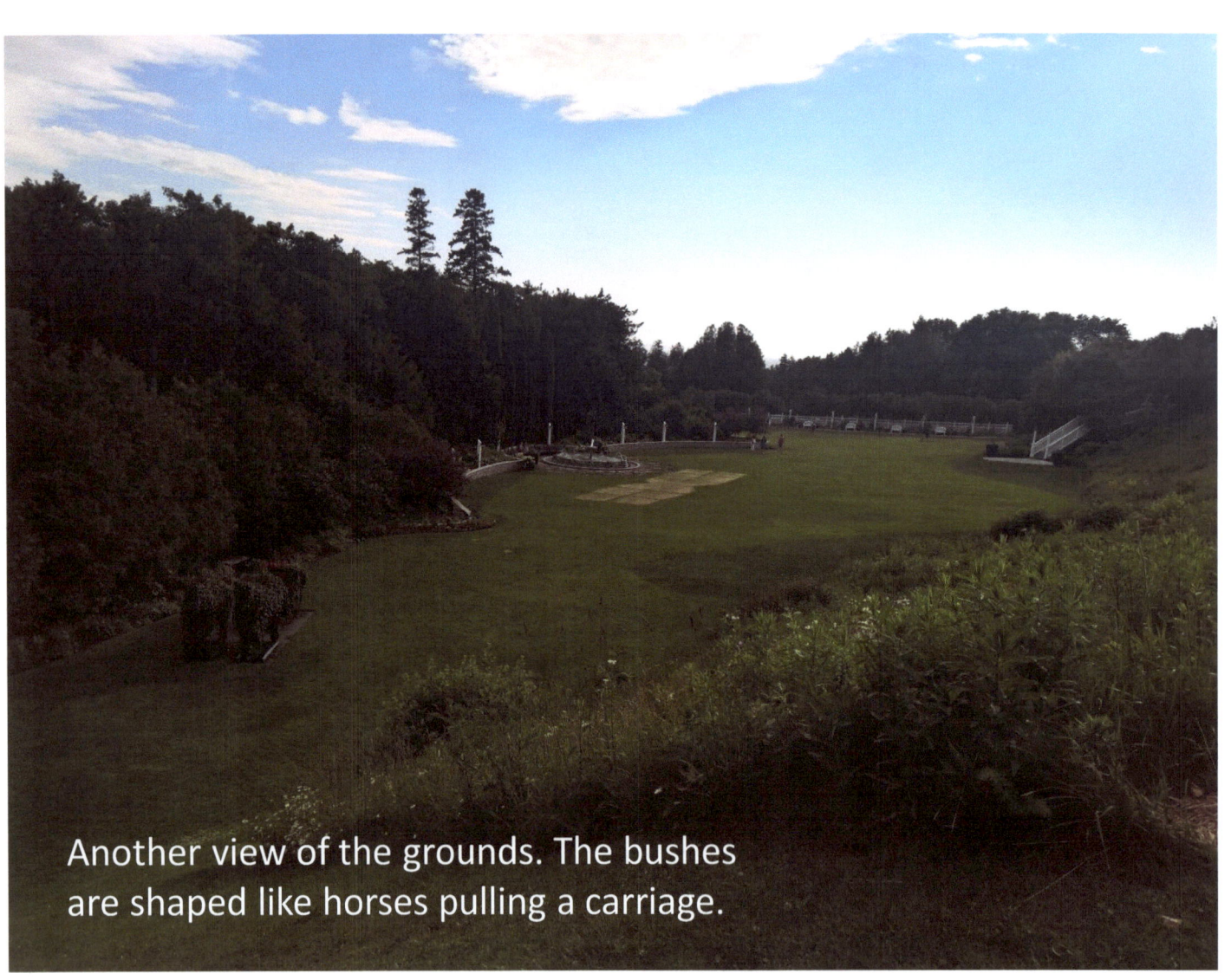

Another view of the grounds. The bushes are shaped like horses pulling a carriage.

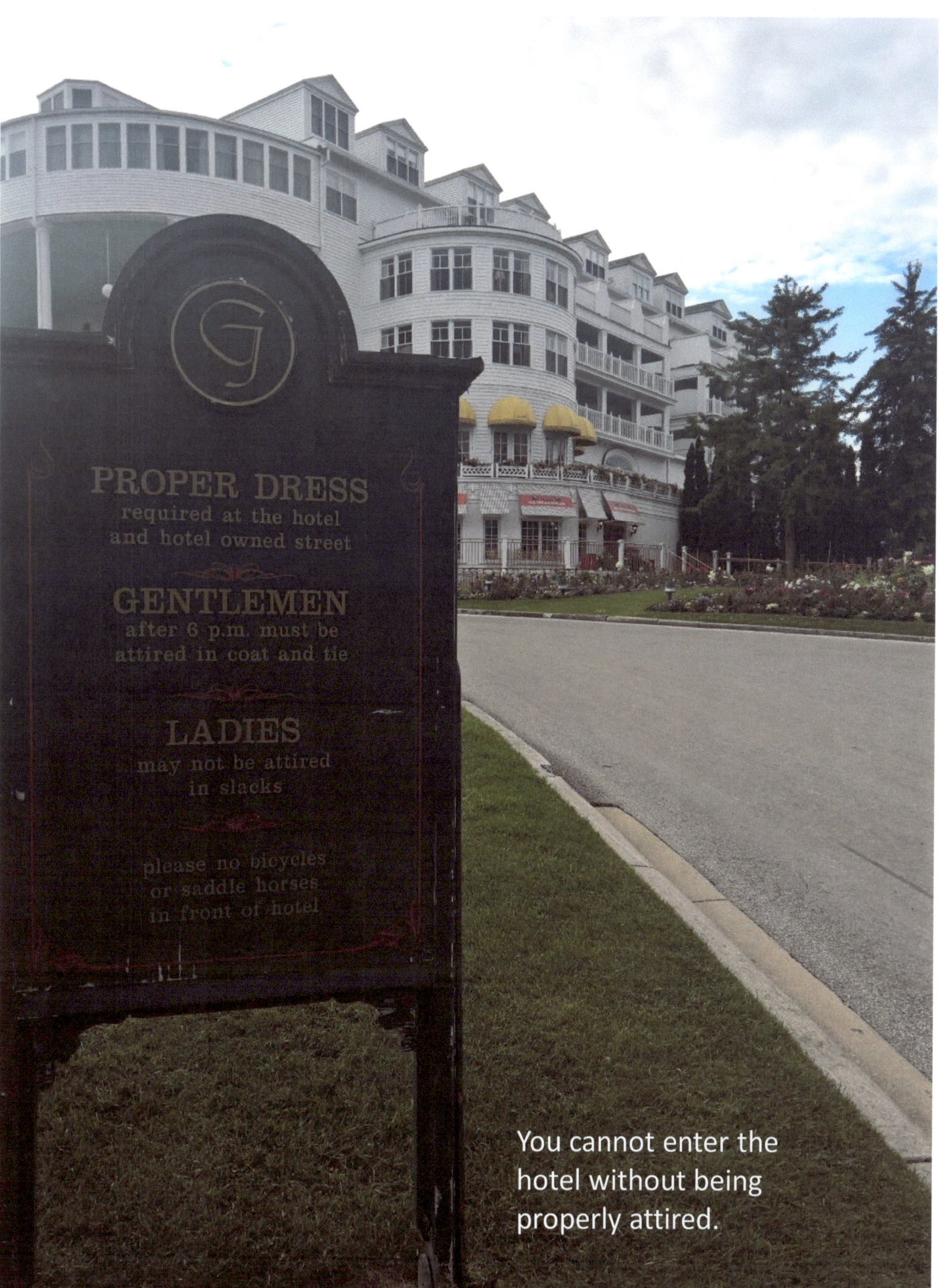

You cannot enter the hotel without being properly attired.

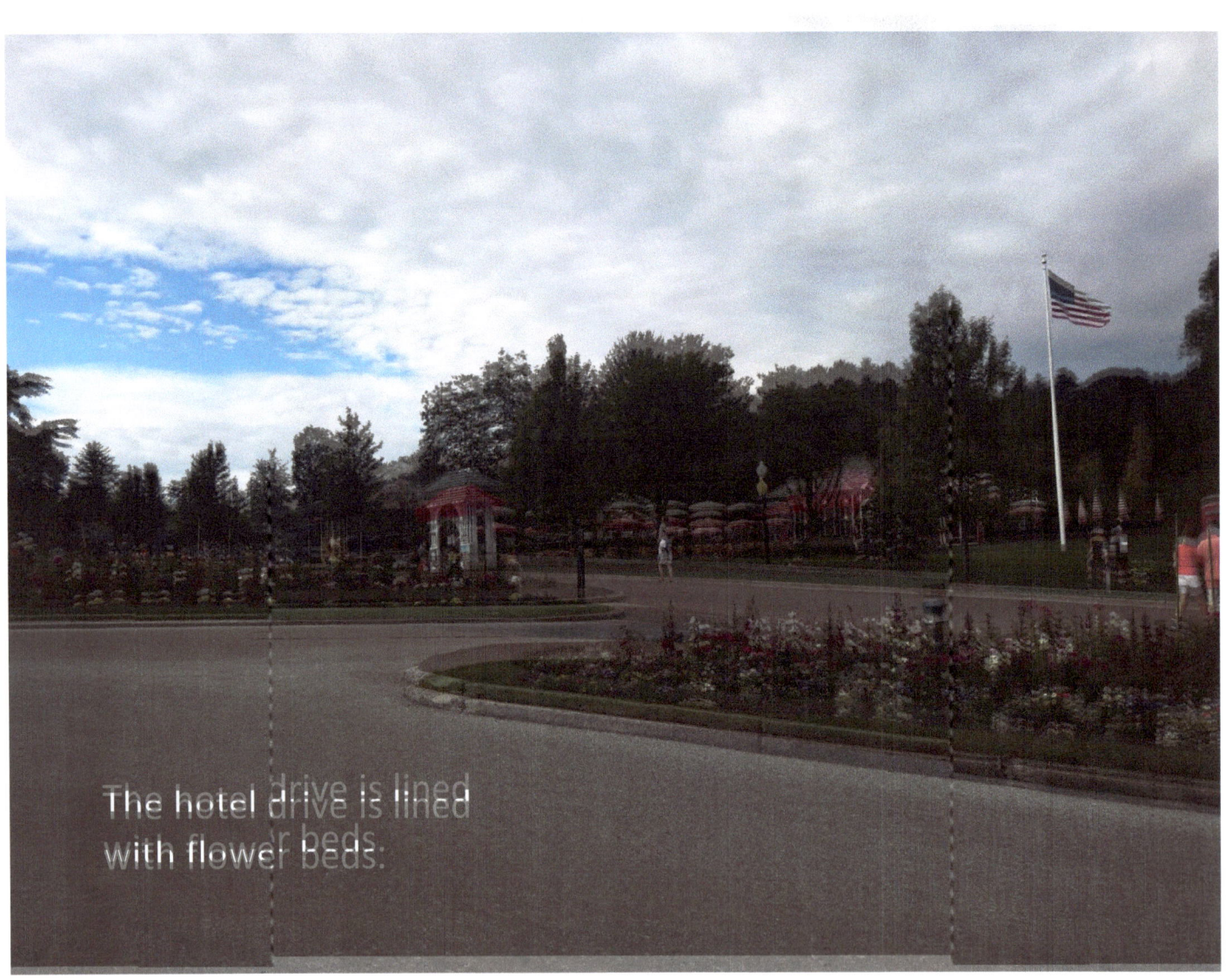

The hotel drive is lined with flower beds.

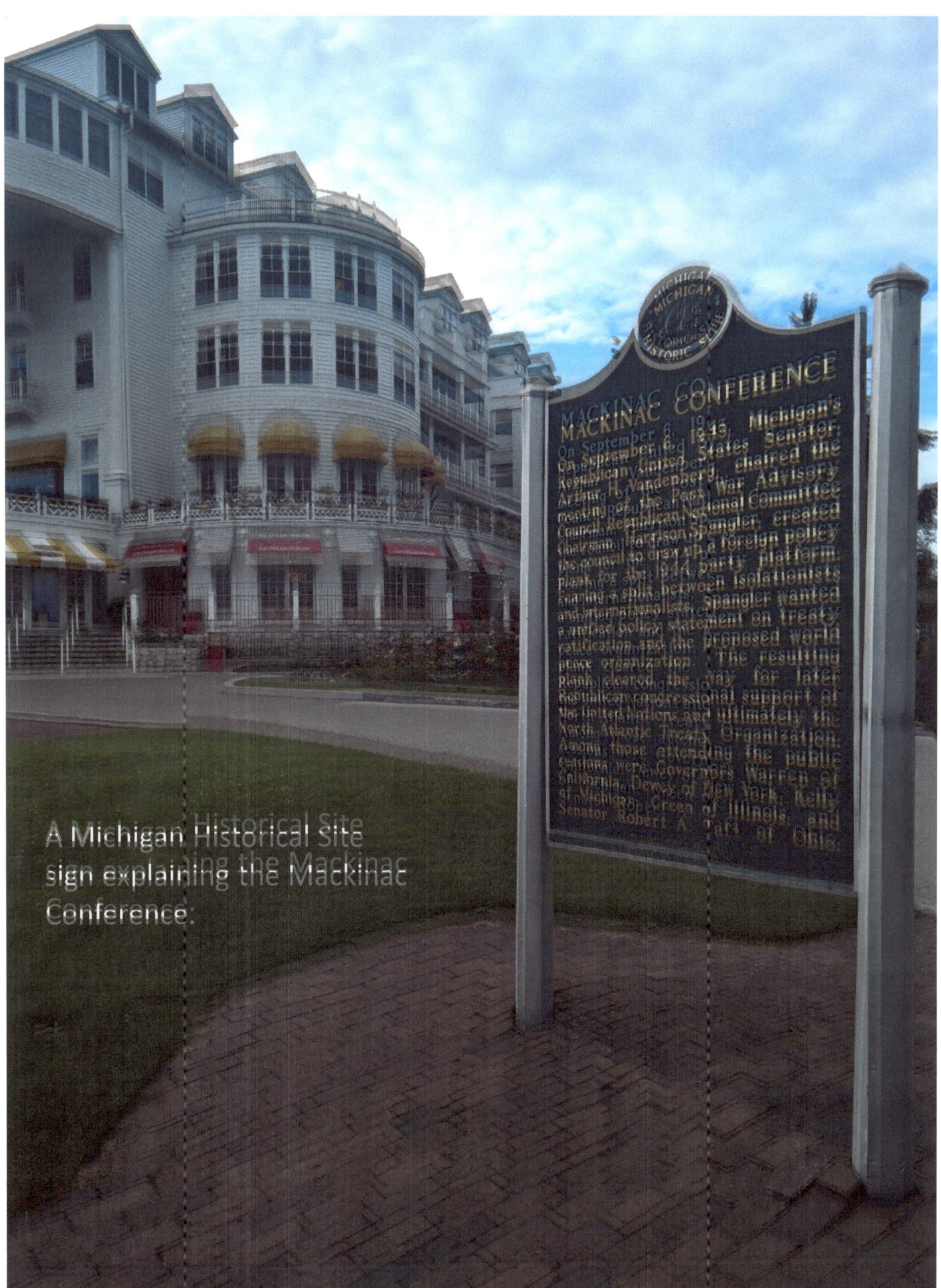

A Michigan Historical Site sign explaining the Mackinac Conference.

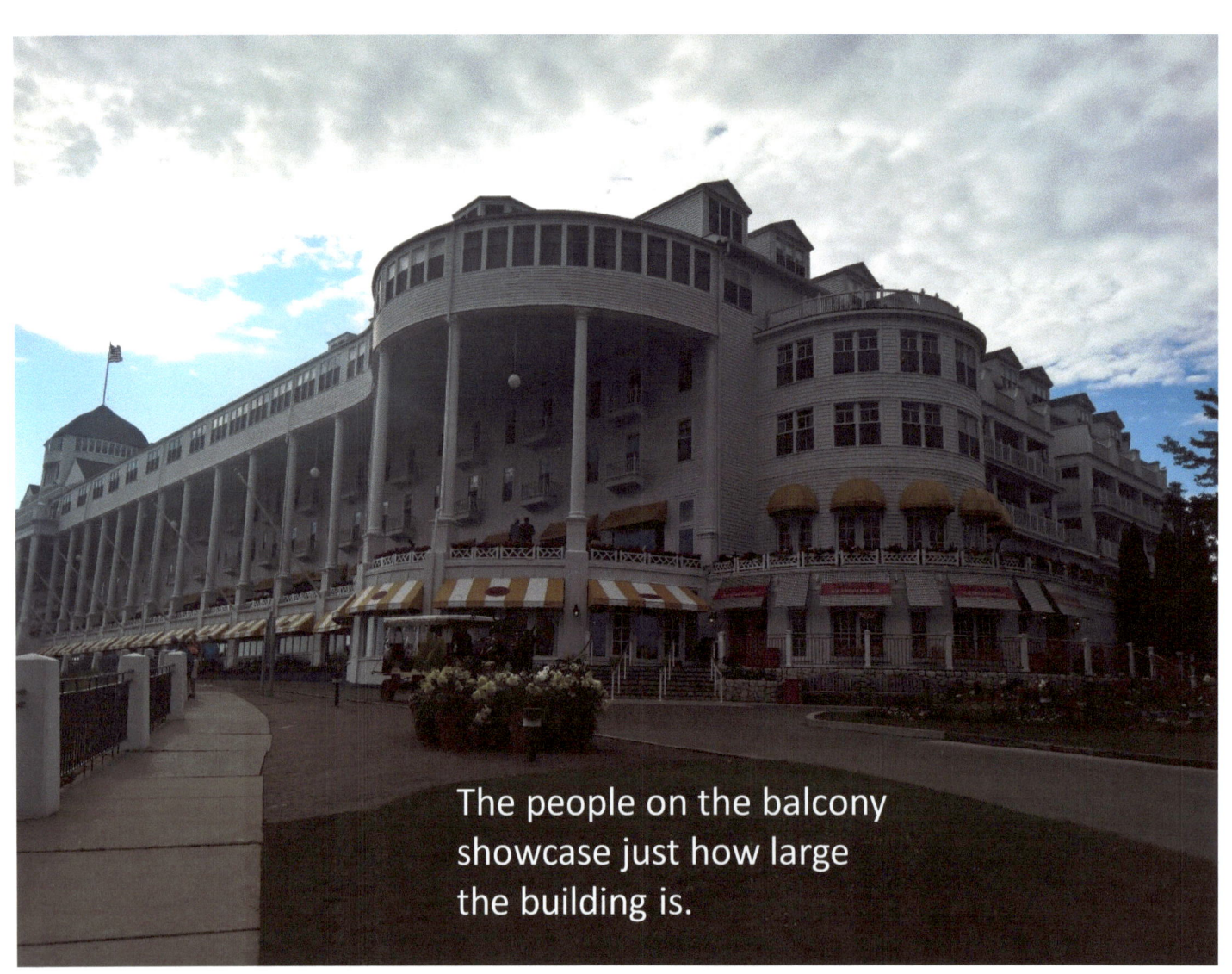

The people on the balcony showcase just how large the building is.

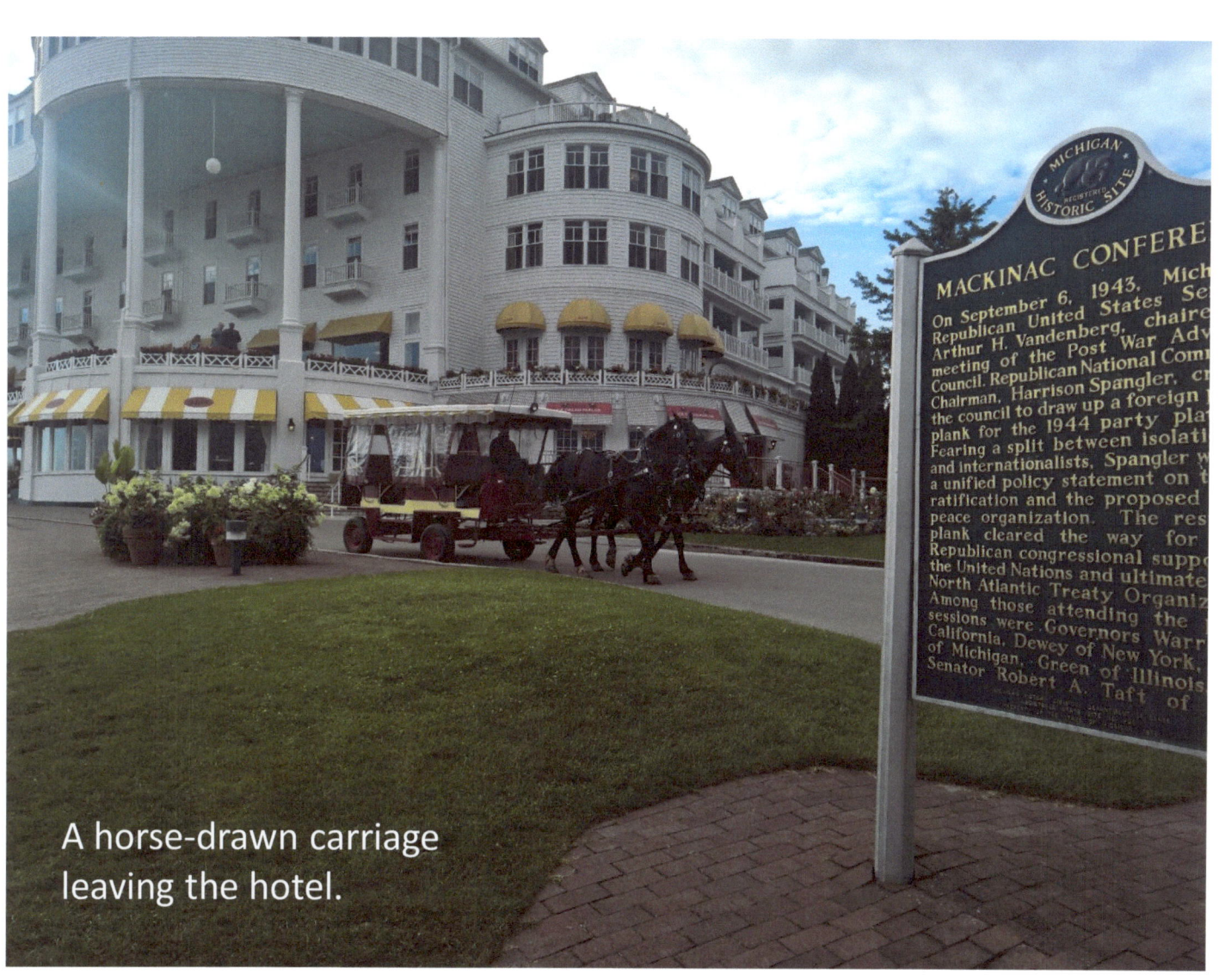

A horse-drawn carriage leaving the hotel.

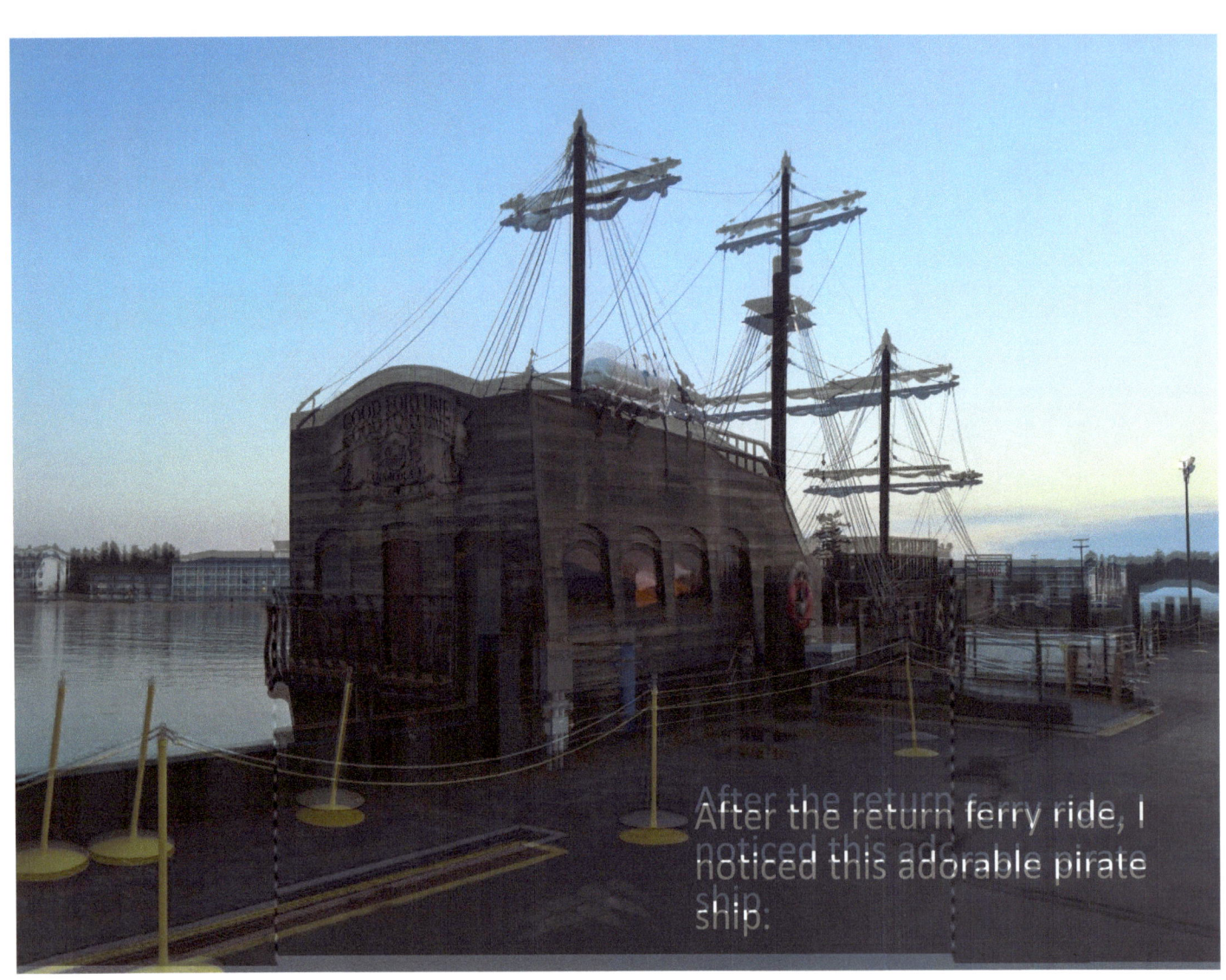
After the return ferry ride, I noticed this adorable pirate ship.

That's all I have for this first volume of Mackinac Island. In an effort to ensure this book stays reasonably sized so that it can be reasonably priced, I've limited this first volume to snapshots and snippets of some of the great things you can see and do on the island.

The images in this book represent just a very small selection of everything on the island. You can rent horses, rent bicycles, stay at one of the many different hotels, get married, have a wedding reception, eat wonderful food, and so much more. The fudge alone is worth visiting for!

I hope the photos I've shared here with you help to give you a general idea of how much fun visiting Mackinac Island can be. You'll find there are tons of comprehensive tour guides, historical books, and website information available as well.

You'll find the official Mackinac Island website at https://www.mackinacisland.org/

Book Summary

One of the frustrating things about EBooks is that it's difficult to remember what they're about after you've purchased them. There is no traditional "back of the book" summary to glance at. This section is designed to help with that.

This is a photo essay, or travel essay, that showcases some of the highlights of Mackinac Island Michigan.

I visited there for the first time in July 2017, with some of my extended family that lives in the area. The island is a wonderful mix of historical buildings, crafts, workshops, reenactments, food, and fun.

There is so much to see and do on the island that it's difficult to fit into one day. This booklet is a mix of my best 50 photos from the historical and notable parts of my visit. My original goal was to see The Grand Hotel, but this booklet also includes snippets from the old Army fort, the infirmary/hospital, the blacksmith's shop, and more.

About the Author
Kathy Burns

Hi there, I'm Kathy :)

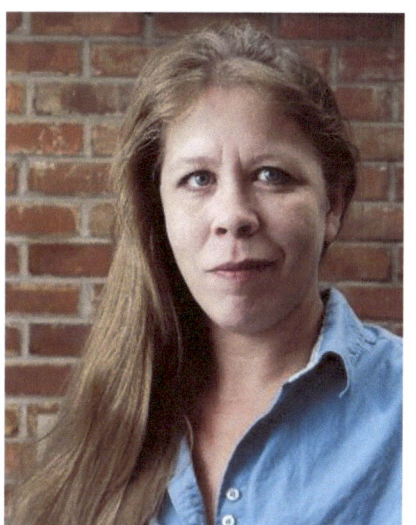

I'm a professional freelance editor, stock photographer, and online publisher who has an avid interest in gardening, photography, and travel.

I've worked from home since 1997, and I've spent most of that time as a freelance business, technical, and marketing writer. In late 2008 I decided to start putting some of my work into Amazon Kindle EBook form.

Now that my children are grown, I focus more on travel and photography instead of writing. I still have older books and guides on Amazon Kindle, and I plan to publish new travel and craft related material from 2018 forward.

As of autumn 2017, I live in the Shenandoah Valley area of Northern Virginia, and am flirting with the idea of traveling the country in a motorhome.

You can find more of my work online at my main website:
ElectronicPerceptions.com

I sometimes publish updates on Instagram:
http://www.instagram.com/SasEzShots

Thank You:

Thank you for buying this Kindle EBook. It is one of several I've published in this format and I have more available on Amazon.

Note: Some of my older books were published under the name 'Kathy Burns-Millyard'.

Please remember to take a moment to leave your comments and reviews at the Amazon Kindle book website so that future buyers can benefit from your thoughts and opinions.

END OF BOOK

www.ingramcontent.com/pod-product-compliance
Lightning Source LLC
Chambersburg PA
CBHW051921210526
45473CB00006B/2097